Understand
Existentialism

Nigel Rodgers and Mel Thompson

D1255939

For UK order enquiries: please contact Bookpoint Ltd,
130 Milton Park, Abingdon, Oxon OX14 4SB.
Telephone: +44 (0) 1235 827720. Fax: +44 (0) 1235 400454.
Lines are open 09.00–17.00, Monday to Saturday, with a 24-hour
message answering service. Details about our titles and how to
order are available at www.teachyourself.com

For USA order enquiries: please contact McGraw-Hill
Customer Services, PO Box 545, Blacklick, OH 43004-0545, USA.
Telephone: 1-800-722-4726. Fax: 1-614-755-5645.

For Canada order enquiries: please contact McGraw-Hill
Ryerson Ltd, 300 Water St, Whitby, Ontario L1N 9B6, Canada.
Telephone: 905 430 5000. Fax: 905 430 5020.

Long renowned as the authoritative source for self-guided
learning – with more than 50 million copies sold worldwide –
the **Teach Yourself** series includes over 500 titles in the fields of
languages, crafts, hobbies, business, computing and education.

British Library Cataloguing in Publication Data: a catalogue record
for this title is available from the British Library.

Library of Congress Catalog Card Number: on file.

First published in UK 2010 by Hodder Education,
part of Hachette UK, 338 Euston Road, London NW1 3BH.

First published in US 2010 by The McGraw-Hill Companies, Inc.

This edition published 2010.

The **Teach Yourself** name is a registered trade mark of
Hodder Headline.

Typeset by MPS Limited, a Macmillan Company.

Printed in Great Britain for Hodder Education, an Hachette UK
Company, 338 Euston Road, London NW1 3BH, by CPI Group
(UK) Ltd, Croydon, CR0 4YY.

The publisher has used its best endeavours to ensure that the URLs
for external websites referred to in this book are correct and active
at the time of going to press. However, the publisher and the author
have no responsibility for the websites and can make no guarantee
that a site will remain live or that the content will remain relevant,
decent or appropriate.

Hachette UK's policy is to use papers that are natural, renewable
and recyclable products and made from wood grown in sustainable
forests. The logging and manufacturing processes are expected to
conform to the environmental regulations of the country of origin.

Impression number   10 9 8 7 6 5 4 3 2

Year   2014 2013

Contents

Credits

Front cover: © Dario Egidi/istockphoto.com

Back cover: © Jakub Semeniuk/iStockphoto.com, © Royalty-Free/Corbis, © agencyby/iStockphoto.com, © Andy Cook/iStockphoto.com, © Christopher Ewing/iStockphoto.com, © zebicho – Fotolia.com, © Geoffrey Holman/iStockphoto.com, © Photodisc/Getty Images, © James C. Pruitt/iStockphoto.com, © Mohamed Saber – Fotolia.com

Meet the authors

Welcome to *Understand Existentialism*!

When I first read Sartre and Camus, I immediately felt that they were writers and thinkers who answered elemental questions – questions that very few other philosophers then seemed prepared to accept as important. Discovering Nietzsche and Dostoyevsky, the 'ancestors' of existentialism soon afterwards, was even more exciting. Nothing I have read since has had the same seismic effect. The perennial *existential* questions — What am I doing here? Has life any meaning? Am I responsible for my actions? – are not just questions for perplexed adolescents. They concern every human being worth the name. As Sartre unforgettably put it, simply through being human we are condemned to be free – an exhilarating but demanding liberty. The answers existentialists proposed were never conventionally comforting. But they remain among the most far-reaching and honest of modern times.

Nigel Rodgers, 2010

I suspect that most of us are existentialists most of the time. Certainly, in my own case, even before studying philosophy, I took to asking what life was for, admired people who seemed to live in an authentic way, unafraid to be themselves, and recognized how easy it was to hide behind social masks. I first encountered existentialism through the writings of the theologian Paul Tillich, who inspired my teenage self to opt to study the philosophy of religion, and then went on to the eye-opening challenge of reading Nietzsche and Kierkegaard. I hope you too will enjoy both studying existentialism as a philosophy, and asking yourself the existential questions – even if it gives you (as it did me) some *Angst* in the process!

Mel Thompson, 2010

Only got a minute?

What is human life about? What does it mean to be an authentic human individual? Am I trapped by the circumstances of my birth, or can I genuinely transcend them? How do I understand and cope with the hopes, fears and anxieties that shape my life?

These are existential questions. They do not require an overall explanation about the nature of reality. Nor can they be answered in scientific terms. Instead, they start with the basic fact that human individuals live in relation to the world around them. People have projects that they seek to fulfil; their choices are based on hopes for the future. Yet life is finite and we face an inevitable death. What, if anything, is therefore worthwhile?

These questions have long been explored through art, literature and religion, but they are also central to one particular tradition in philosophy: existentialism. It considers the meaning of human life: its goals, significance and the experience of responsibility – shaping the future and living in an authentic way. In other words, it is about what it means to be a human being living in the world. *The general view of existentialist philosophers is that life is not presented to us already packaged with meaning and purpose, but it is what we make of it.*

Existentialism became hugely popular in Europe in the years following the Second World War, when people were all too aware of the fragility of life and wanted a philosophy that was positive, self-affirming but not escapist. Whether it has a renewed relevance for the second decade of the twenty-first century, when economic, political, social and environmental issues continue to confront people with an uncertain future, is for you to judge.

5 Only got five minutes?

Although questions about human life and its meaning have regularly been explored in religion, philosophy and literature, they also became central to a group of writers, philosophers and artists who came to be called 'existentialists'. In post-war Paris existentialism, centred on the work of Jean-Paul Sartre, became probably the most fashionable philosophy known. With it came a belief in freedom and self-determination and the rejection of convention.

Let us, for now, examine just a few of its key features:

Actors, not observers...

Existentialism is a deeply human philosophy. It starts from the point of view that the world is not something 'out there' that we observe and about which we speculate, but that in which we live. That is the defining sense of existentialism – it is about engagement with the world, rather than analysis. Existentialists were concerned to get away from any sense (for which they tended to blame the philosopher Descartes and his claim 'I think, therefore I am') that a person is no more than his or her thoughts. Life is about acting, making choices, using things that come to hand as tools, exploring relationships and the effect they have on you. You cannot understand life by standing back and observing it; you understand it only in engagement.

Essence and existence...

If we were tools, manufactured for particular purposes, we would have our essence predetermined. To use an example that goes right back to Aristotle, a good knife is one that cuts well, because the essence of a knife is cutting. Know the essence of a tool and you know how best to use it. But do I have some predetermined essence? Do I behave as I do because I am a certain sort of person? Or do I shape the sort of person I am by the choices I make? For existentialists the latter is the case. The famous expression of Sartre 'existence precedes essence' effectively defines existentialism. In human life, essence is shaped by existence, not the other way round.

Living forwards...

We are always planning, looking forward to things. Our mind is filled with the 'not yet' that we want to bring about, and this moment vanishes immediately into a past that is 'no longer'. Yet neither the future nor the past, although they are utterly important to us and define our lives, actually exists in the present except by way of anticipation or memory. To exist means (literally) to 'stand out' – and when it comes to human existence, the key feature is that we are always going out of ourselves, looking for something, planning, organizing the future.

Freedom and responsibility...

Existentialism challenges us to take responsibility for ourselves and for the life we choose to lead. It also insists that we are free, whether we like it or not. We cannot determine the circumstances in which we find ourselves, but we are free (with no opt-out, 'condemned to be free' in Sartre's terms) to decide how we are going to understand and respond to them. I may blame others for the circumstances in which I find myself, but I cannot blame them for the choices I make. I have to take responsibility for my own life.

So exploring existentialism is unlike a study of any other branch of philosophy. It is more of a personal quest and challenge, more immediately related to the arts, to ethics and to questions of personal meaning, direction and significance.

10 Only got ten minutes?

Existentialism is about the experience of living as a human being. It is about engaging with the world and dealing with two features of life – the situation in which we find ourselves and the constant desire to go beyond ourselves, planning and shaping our future.

As such, its interest is very different from that of traditional metaphysics, which asks questions about the most general principles and truths, or science, which examines and gives objective information about the world. If anything, it is nearer to religion, in that it explores the meaning of human life as it is lived, although existentialists were divided between those (Buber, Marcel, Jaspers) who were religious – even if unconventionally so – and those (Sartre, de Beauvoir, Camus) who were atheist. But unlike most religious traditions, it does not attempt to base its view of life on any general, metaphysical principles or speculative ideas. Rather, it discovers (or creates) values and meanings in the process of living.

It is not only a philosophy but a way of life, a way of exploring in the arts and literature, and a form of self-affirmation that has profound ethical consequences. It is also a philosophy of freedom and of responsibility – challenging the individual to shape his or her own life, acknowledging uniqueness rather than trying to escape into social conformity.

To anyone who might think that philosophy is about abstract and unworldly speculation and logic, with picking apart arguments and disputing the use of terms, then existentialism will come as a breath of philosophical fresh air. There is nothing more relevant to any human being than the existential questions, for they set our personal agenda.

The context

Every philosophy arises against a background in thought and in history. The precursors and founding fathers of existentialist thought: Pascal, Kierkegaard, Dostoyevsky, Nietzsche and Kafka, probed existential questions in their writings, and themselves reflected a longer history, which goes back to St Augustine, to Plato, even to Lao Tzu and the Buddha.

But existentialism, as it emerged in the 1940s, depended on other thinkers earlier in the twentieth century, who provided much of its groundwork. The phenomenology of Husserl opened up a way of philosophizing on experience itself, of seeing how all our experience comes with purpose and intention attached. Then Heidegger – although he refused to accept the label 'existentialist' – produced *Being and Time*, one of the masterpieces of twentieth-century thought. In this, he fleshed out a study of Dasein, the individual human presence in the world, introducing many of the key features of existentialism.

At the same time, Karl Jaspers, drawing from his twin interests of psychology and philosophy, introduced a philosophy of *Existenz*, and Martin Buber, in his profoundly religious work *I and Thou*, explored the fundamental difference between engagement with the world of persons and the world of things.

But perhaps the most obvious and immediate context for the development of existentialism was the Second World War. Sartre developed the key themes for his major work of existentialist philosophy, *Being and Nothingness*, while in a German prisoner-of-war camp, and returned to Paris to work alongside the Resistance. It was a world where issues of courage and cowardice, or personal integrity and play-acting, were all the more real because the consequences of decisions were so immediate and potentially fatal. It was a world dominated by the great ideologies – Fascism, Communism, Democracy – for which people gave their lives, but also one in which the limitations of those same ideologies were all too obvious.

At the end of the war, surrounded by reminders of the horrors of death and privation, people were just beginning to learn the scale of the Holocaust and coming to terms with the use of the atomic bomb.

In those grim days, the question was not just 'Why?' but also 'What now?' How can I make sense of my life if it is always subject to random destruction? Is life really absurd? Does anything matter? Existentialism promised to rise to that challenge, to offer a philosophy of hope that did not try to dodge the issues.

The style

Existentialism thrived as literature and art, as well as philosophy. If you want to explore what it is to be confronted with the responsibility of radical freedom, to shape your future and live an authentic life, it can be easier to do so through fiction or theatre than by reading philosophy. Novels such as Camus' *The Outsider*, or Sartre's *Nausea*, address and explore these issues in a way that is real, immediate and utterly jargon free. There aren't many areas of philosophy where that can be said.

Existentialism quickly became fashionable as a lifestyle: unconventional, with no fixed values, no God, and absolute freedom to accept the responsibility of creating one's own sense of direction and value. There was a sense, in those heady days when existentialism was first in fashion, that the old world of convention, metaphysics, established authority and unquestioning obedience had gone. To be an existentialist was to be a very new kind of person.

Key themes

In the previous summary we already mentioned some of these: that existentialism is a philosophy of engagement; that existence comes before essence; that we live forwards; that we are both free and responsible. But let us review four themes that characterize existentialism:

1 Existentialism goes beyond the subject/object divide.
   The world has traditionally been divided up into two very different realms – the subjective and the objective. Some of what I know of life is down to me: my senses, my intuitions, my personal views; other things are objective: space, time and

causality and the whole physical realm over which I seem to have only limited control. But existentialism gets entirely beyond this view of a subjective self looking out onto an objective world. For Heidegger and others, the human world is one that is very different from the world of science; it is a world of personal engagement, of the interpretation of time in terms of the influences of my past and my hopes for the future. From an existentialist point of view, what counts is the experience of life as it is lived.

2 Existentialism is concerned with authentic living.
If we are free and without excuse, we are responsible for the decisions we make. It is a responsibility from which we might seek to escape by adopting a particular role in life, a mask that prevents us from questioning who we are. But to do that is to fall into what Sartre calls 'bad faith'. He gives a wonderful example of a waiter whose actions are all a bit too mannered and contrived, who is clearly trying to be a perfect waiter, rather than just being himself doing his job as well as he can.

To avoid taking up such a role, or hiding behind a mask, involves creating one's own direction and values, rather than accepting those that are ready provided. Authenticity doesn't come easily. Existentialism makes the fundamental distinction between things and consciousness, but is aware that, at any time, a consciousness may choose to see itself as a thing, or may be regarded as a 'thing' by someone else. I may see myself as no more than 'a waiter', and someone else may treat me as nothing but a waiter – in both cases, the unique consciousness is ignored and allowed to merge into the world of objects.

3 Existentialism starts with the individual.
Existentialism is sometimes criticized for placing too much emphasis on the individual and not enough on the influence of the social or political group. This is partly true, particularly of Sartre's writings in the 1940s, where he focuses on the responsibility and inescapable freedom of each individual. But existentialism as a whole was not exclusively individualist.

Sartre moved increasingly towards Marxist communism, eventually seeing existentialism as a subordinate ideology within the overall Marxist critique of society, and even before that, his two closest fellow existentialist thinkers, de Beauvoir and Merleau-Ponty, gave greater emphasis to the social aspects of human life. Indeed, for de Beauvoir, the transformation of the lives of women requires a change in society as well as in the lives of individuals.

4   Existentialism evades definition.

Although there are a number of thinkers who tend to be labelled 'existentialist', there was never any single definition of existentialism. Take Heidegger, for example. His philosophy raises all the key questions that were explored by Sartre and others, such as the experience of being embedded in life, authenticity, taking responsibility for decisions about the possibilities that life offers, and even the central view that existence precedes essence. Yet he did not see himself as an existentialist, for his task was a broader one of trying to understand the nature of being. He used human existential experience as a vehicle for doing so, but not as an end in itself.

So, rather than attempt to see existentialism as a philosophy, it might be better to see it as a set of reactions against traditional philosophical views. In particular, the feeling on the part of Sartre and others was that traditional philosophy was remote from ordinary human life and concerns.

In studying existentialism, it is best to approach it with an open mind and to resist the temptation to expect that its every claim should be defined with absolute clarity. Few today would claim to be existentialists in any formal or exclusive sense, but that is all to the good, for those who try to adopt the label 'existentialist' may be doing no more than using it as a mask. What matters, and why existentialism has a great deal to contribute, is that *the existential questions still need to be asked*.

1

Introduction to existentialism

In this chapter you will learn:

- *about the political and social background to existentialism*
- *why existentialists rejected convention*
- *that existentialism embraced philosophy, art and literature*

Man is nothing else but what he makes of himself. That is the first principle of existentialism.
Until recently philosophers were attacked only by other philosophers. The public understood nothing of it and cared less. Now, however, they have made philosophy come right down into the market place.

Jean-Paul Sartre *Existentialism and Humanism*

Why study existentialism today? Why study philosophy at all? Too often in the past philosophy has sounded like an intellectual debate of academic interest only. Fundamental, pressing questions – 'What is human life about? Why are we what we are? What does it mean to be an *authentic* individual?' – were ignored by many philosophers in the mid-twentieth century in favour of the analytic clarification of language, the critical evaluation of evidence and similar topics seemingly remote from people's experience of life. To find answers, we had had to turn to literature, art or religion.

Unless, that is, the philosophers concerned were existentialists. Existentialists differed radically from many earlier (and later) thinkers in their concern with the present world. The most famous existentialists – Jean-Paul Sartre, Albert Camus, Simone de Beauvoir – were not academics but writers. They lived and worked in Parisian cafés, arguing, drinking and thinking amid the hubbub of everyday life. This now clichéd image contains a central truth. Existentialists confronted the pressing issues of their age and attempted to find answers drawn from experience, not abstract reason. They looked at the whole of human life, its goals, significance and responsibilities – in other words, what it means to be a human being alive in the world.

Existentialism sees life not as coming ready-programmed by some higher power (God, history, evolution, a divine playwright) with meaning and purpose, but being what we ourselves make of it as individuals. It is a philosophy for the brave, the independently-minded. The existentialists themselves were such passionate individualists, frequently disagreeing with each other, that many denied belonging to a movement at all.

Unlike all other creatures (as far as we know) humans are able to ask about the meaning of their lives – not immediately pressing questions about where the next meal is coming from, or how to successfully mate with a suitable partner, but about whether anything in life makes sense. We may be plagued with depression, with doubt. We may pause and not know what to choose. We may be confused, recognizing the freedom to opt for a whole range of different things in life.

Existentialist attitudes are not restricted to the mid-twentieth century. Precursors can be traced back to the very first philosophers, tough-minded ancient Greeks such as Empedocles, Socrates and Diogenes. They too lived, thought and taught philosophy in the dusty streets of their cities, not in academic seclusion. Revealingly, existentialism has given its name to an attitude: 'existential'.

Insight

Stoicism and Platonism have also given their name to attitudes, but logical positivism and post-structuralism have not. This says something about the personal usefulness of different approaches to philosophy.

Existentialism conquered Paris with startling suddenness in 1945, the year after the city's liberation from Nazi rule. Artists, writers, actors and students began calling themselves existentialists, although not all of them would have read *Being and Nothingness*, (*L'Etre et le Néant*) Jean-Paul Sartre's weighty masterpiece published in 1943. In September 1945 Simone de Beauvoir, Sartre's one-time lover and lifelong collaborator, published her novel *The Blood of Others* (*Le Sang des Autres*), exploring quintessentially existentialist themes of freedom and **responsibility**. So did her play that opened that summer. In October the first issue of *Les Temps Modernes* ('Modern Times', echoing Charlie Chaplin's film), appeared with Sartre and his colleague Merleau-Ponty as editors. It became the age's foremost intellectual magazine, gaining a wide readership.

Also that October, Sartre delivered his lecture 'Existentialism is a humanism' ('*L'Existentialisme est un Humanisme*'), attracting such a large audience that some of his listeners fainted in the crush. The first two of his trilogy of novels *The Roads to Freedom* (*Les Chemins de la Liberté*) appeared in 1945. *The Outsider* (*L'Etranger*), a novel, and *The Myth of Sisyphus* (*Le Mythe de Sisyphe*), both written by Albert Camus during the war, also became bestsellers. Although there were other important existentialist thinkers, none quite matched Sartre, de Beauvoir and Camus in combining their three-fold roles as writers, as thinkers and as human beings committed to political action.

For Parisians of the post-war years – hungry, cold, exhausted, horrified by seeing the first films of the Nazi death camps in April 1945 and then learning of the nuclear bombs dropped on Hiroshima and Nagasaki in August – existentialism was no mere affectation. It offered a way of understanding and facing the traumas of the modern world. As de Beauvoir put it, a generation 'had lost their faith in perpetual peace, in eternal progress, in unchanging essences... They had discovered History in its most terrible form. They needed an ideology which would include such revelations... Existentialism, struggling to reconcile history and morality, gave them authority to accept their transitory condition... to face horror and absurdity while still retaining their human dignity, to preserve their individuality' (*Force of Circumstance*, 1965).

> De Beauvoir's words sum up existentialism's appeal and essence. It was a *humanizing* philosophy for a dehumanized age, a time of crisis and extremes, when the traditional philosophical approaches appeared a redundant luxury.

Existentialism as a philosophy has had a huge impact on the worlds of literature, art and theatre. This was not the case with English Empiricism, logical positivism or Linguistic Analysis. Unlike these schools of thoughts, existentialism reached out to challenge and affect all aspects of human life.

Since Plato banished poets and painters from his ideal Republic, many philosophers have shied away from artists and writers, regarding them as unreliable bohemians. Not so the existentialists. The isolated, emaciated figures of Alberto Giacometti (1901–66) suggest existentialist tension and tragedy. Giacometti indeed portrayed Simone de Beauvoir while Sartre wrote enthusiastically on Giacometti's work, notably the introduction to the exhibition in New York in 1948 that established the artist's fame. In Beckett's *Waiting for Godot (En attendant Godot)*, first performed in 1953, the two tramps inhabit a desolate void that is indeed existentialist.

If existentialism's artistic lineage can be traced back through the surrealists and Dadaists to the cubists, its literary ancestors include Franz Kafka and Alfred Jarry. But existentialism has the most impressive philosophical ancestry too. Paradoxically, for a movement that was so French and centred on Paris, most of its intellectual ancestors were Germans – Søren Kierkegaard was Danish, but nineteenth-century Denmark lay in Germany's intellectual shadow. The movement's unwilling father was Martin Heidegger (1889–1976), considered one of the twentieth century's two greatest philosophers (the other being Ludwig Wittgenstein). Heidegger's teacher and mentor was Edmund Husserl, his colleague Karl Jaspers – all Germans. Behind Heidegger, half-acknowledged, stood the prophetic figure of Friedrich Nietzsche, very German despite himself.

With such ancestors, existentialism in 1945 was ready to rock.

Above all else, existentialism is concerned with the whole of human experience – thinking, feeling, acting, engaging in the world. It is not detached or objective. It does not seek to construct an abstract system to explain everything; indeed, it is suspicious of all such systems. It starts with humankind – from birth to death, a life that is bounded by physical circumstances and constraints, but which also aspires to freedom, to choosing and shaping values, to transcending its present self to become something more in the future, to making sense of a life that is inevitably heading towards death.

Existentialists thought that philosophy should relate to life, to the ordinary concerns and decisions that people face. They rejected the notion of philosophy as a matter of intellectual speculation about the meaning of things in general; for them thought should always be embedded in human experience.

Some (e.g. Walter Kaufmann, writing in 1975) rejected the idea of existentialism as a single philosophy, seeing it as a label that can be given to a range of very different reactions against traditional philosophy. This is even more the case when we explore existentialism in its broadest sense – from philosophy, to literature, theatre and the fine arts. Existentialism is a phenomenon rather than a school of thought. Do not expect to find a single set of principles accepted by all existentialist thinkers.

What's in a name?

Existentialism is a problematic title. The writer Gabriel Marcel used it of Sartre, who first rejected it, but then decided to embrace it and define it in a famous lecture in 1945, now reproduced in a little book entitled *Existentialism and Humanism*. So one option would be to take Sartre's philosophy as the norm for existentialism. But that would not do justice to the range of ideas that comprise what we generally think of as existentialism.

Heidegger, for example, rejected the term 'existentialist' for his philosophy. Yet Sartre, while in a prisoner-of-war camp, spent his time studying Heidegger's major work *Being and Time*, many themes of which Sartre took up in his own philosophy.

By 1945 Maurice Merleau-Ponty – a friend and fellow student of Sartre and de Beauvoir's – was able (in his *The Phenomenology of Perception*, 1945) to speak of existentialism as if it were an established tradition. As early as 1919, the philosopher and psychologist Karl Jaspers (1883–1969) had used the term *Existenz Philosophie* for his exploration of existentialist themes. But it was only after being accepted by Sartre, that existentialism became the general term for the approach of those thinkers who were concerned with what Heidegger called Dasein – human life engaged with its world. And once that name was established, it began to gather about itself a whole range of philosophers, writers and artists who shared its values, soon becoming a slogan for a social movement that embraced freedom and rejection of convention.

So there was never a single, fixed view of existentialism. That should come as no surprise, for it is curious that existential thinkers should want to coin the term 'existentialism' at all. As we shall see later, Sartre's principal existentialist doctrine is that 'existence precedes essence'. In other words, what you do shapes what you are, not the other way around. Hence it is important to see that there is no hidden essence called 'existentialism' to which thinkers were invited to subscribe. Rather, they approached a common set of questions and areas of interest centred on what it means to be a human being in the world as we know and experience it: the dilemmas of everyday life, the questions of meaning and value and determining what is worth doing.

Insight

Apart from anything else, the label 'existentialist' tended to imply a radical break from tradition, and a measure of personal freedom that would have alienated many conventional thinkers.

Do not expect from existentialism a single, coherent system of thought, explaining everything. That is not its style. Think of it as the thoughts of a group of philosophers, writers and artists who, confronted with the tyranny of organized, systematized, scientific and quasi-scientific thought, rebelled in the name of humanity. They sought to explore what it means to be human, how to understand the issues of life, death and personal meaning, what it is to have a past and to anticipate a future, what it means to be committed, or to be concerned, to create and live by values. But it also acknowledges the sense that, alone and frighteningly free in a vast, meaningless world, humankind experiences that profound uncertainty which is given the name 'angst'. **Angst** starts to appear when we stop our routine obedience to the formulas given to us by society and tradition and start to ask 'What's it all for?'

Doing it the continental way...

Philosophy departments in Britain and the United States hardly mentioned existentialism at the time (1945–60) when it was at its most fashionable in Paris. Indeed, many books that give an outline of philosophy for those thinking of studying the subject at university include, at most, a chapter on 'continental philosophy'. It is therefore important to appreciate the way in which continental philosophy became different from the Anglo-American analytic tradition.

Two questions dominated much Anglo-American philosophy for most of the twentieth century, both of them associated with Wittgenstein.

The first concerns evidence and factual meaning, arising from the work of the logical positivist movement in the 1920s and 1930s. The logical positivists (themselves first based in Vienna, disproving too geographical an interpretation of the split within philosophy between analytic and continental) wanted to give philosophy the precision of science. Impressed by Wittgenstein's *Tractatus*, they wanted to make language transparent to evidence. A statement was factually true if it could be backed by evidence, false if evidence went against it. And any statements for which there was no relevant evidence, could not be factually meaningful. In other words, if you make a claim, it can only be said to be true or false if you can specify what evidence would count for or against it. This, of course, created problems for moral and religious statements, neither of which seemed susceptible to evidential proof or disproof. It also ruled out most of the questions with which existentialist thinkers were concerned.

The second concerned the nature and use of language. In his later work, Wittgenstein argued that the meaning of language is found in its use. Language is developed by particular groups of people for a particular function, and its meaning is given by the way they use it. This was significantly different from the earlier phase of seeking evidence for the meaningfulness of statements.

But the result of these two trends was to see the function of philosophy as being that of clarification. Philosophers were not expected to have anything to say about real life – political options, moral dilemmas and so on. Their task was far more remote and abstract: to clarify the meaning of words and the validity of arguments. But they might make no value judgements, nor put out theories that might send youth to the barricades. They certainly did not consider it the responsibility of philosophy to shape a cultural rebellion. While the analytic tradition of philosophy sought clarity, the continentals sought meaning.

That makes for objectivity, detachment and precision in language. But it does not accommodate the sort of general questions about meaning and purpose with which existentialists have been concerned. These are not questions that can be answered in terms of evidence.

Thus, for much philosophy as it was taught in universities in Britain and the United States during much of the twentieth century, the question about the nature and meaning of life as we experience it (the question at the heart of existentialism) is simply a non-question.

Insight

The existentialist philosophers claimed that the analytic tradition of assuming that thinkers can take a detached, external view of the world, is mistaken. *They were interested in the questions arising from being in the world, not from attempting to get an external, objective view of the world.*

Now much of this would seem to be obvious. If you are asked to describe your experience of being a member of the human species living in the world today, you do not start by ordering a brainscan, or trying to check whether your senses give an accurate representation of features of the world around you? Better that you describe the circumstances of your life, where you were born, where you live and so on. These are the physical facts of your life. But you would also want to express your hopes and fears – thinking about what does not yet exist. Your life might have two kinds of explanation. One, looking back, would give causal explanations for how you came to be where you are today, and the other, looking forward, would express the projects and plans that give your life meaning and significance for you. As Heidegger described it, we live life forwards, always choosing what we want to happen.

So there is a fundamental choice to be made – either you accept that philosophy can explore the experience of engaged living, dealing with issues such as anxiety, freedom, hope and so on, or else you limit it to logic, language and the checking of empirical facts. In the first, knowledge comes by way of reflecting on one's participation in the world; in the second it comes by observation of the world, setting aside (as far as possible) one's own subjectivity. Existentialism opted for the former, while the philosophy of the English-speaking world, through much of the twentieth century, generally opted for the latter.

On from the 1940s?

The existentialists of the 1940s and 50s might have looked a free-living, unconventional, even hedonistic and anti-authoritarian bunch. Some people may have been attracted to existentialism for just those reasons. Yet beneath that there is a seriousness and commitment to create value and meaning in a world from which the old certainties have vanished.

Post-modernism and structuralism in time supplanted existentialism as a fashionable philosophical position. By the 1950s Sartre and others were already seeing it as a limited ideology serving the dominant philosophy of the time – Marxism. But the world continues to pose existential questions, life is as uncertain as ever and science, for all its advances, has not provided answers to fundamental questions about the experience of being human. So the issues with which the existentialists grappled are still with us.

Of course, to appreciate its present relevance, we need to distinguish existential philosophy from the cultural phenomenon of permissive self-affirmation, struggling to say something exciting and positive against a backdrop of desperate hardships and **nihilism** of post-war Europe. It was the latter which launched existentialism as a fashionable set of ideas with lifestyle attached. The former, as we shall see, has much deeper roots, in questions that were being asked long before Sartre emerged before the crowds in 1945.

Nevertheless, there will always be one character who embodies a line of enquiry more than any other. And in this case it is indeed Sartre – sitting forward across a table, cigarette in hand, expounding his views, in Paris in the years following the Second World War. It was from that particular time and place that existentialism emerged to become a general term for a cultural trend and way of life. Existentialism is what happens when philosophy hits the streets and engages with the questions thrown up by ordinary life.

10 THINGS TO REMEMBER

1 *Key existentialists were writers rather than professional academics.*

2 *Existentialism came to the fore and flourished in post-war Paris.*

3 *It addressed the question of personal meaning in a traumatized world.*

4 *Existentialism influenced (and developed within) the arts and literature.*

5 *Existentialists rebelled against conventional thinking.*

6 *Existentialism draws on the writings of Kierkegaard and Nietzsche.*

7 *Existentialism is concerned with lived experience, not abstract speculation.*

8 *Existentialism contrasts with most English-speaking twentieth-century philosophy.*

9 *Existentialism is not a single, defined school of thought.*

10 *The relevance of existentialism lies in its questions as much as its answers.*

2

Living dangerously: the roots of
existentialism

In this chapter you will learn:

- *that existentialism had many precursors dating back to
  the 17th century*
- *that all existentialists believed in living their philosophy,
  even if it endangered them.*

> *There is but one truly serious philosophical problem and that is
> suicide. Judging whether life is or is not worth living amounts to
> answering the fundamental question of philosophy.*
>
> Albert Camus *The Myth of Sisyphus* (1942)

Anyone looking to existentialism for the consolations of eternal
truths will be disappointed. It does not provide any sort of
philosophical comfort blanket. Nor does it offer the quasi-scientific
certainties of the logical positivists and other twentieth-century
analytical schools. Mathematics and logic, often considered central
to philosophy, are ignored by existentialists. They reject the
philosophical approach pioneered by René Descartes (1596–1650).
Descartes famously declared, '*Cogito ergo sum*', 'I think therefore
I am'. By doing so he established the concept of the individual
mind that looks at the world like a spectator at a cinema screen
or as if through a lens.

This method, if effective at solving some philosophical – and many scientific – problems, has led Western thinking into an impasse from which it has needed repeated rescuing. It ignores the fact that the cogitating spectator is also a human being who is born, suffers and dies. Such 'existential' facts shape the way we experience the world. If the existentialists manage to escape Cartesian sterility, their approach demands the intellectual courage to make hard choices, often going against the flow. Only by exercising this freedom can human beings become fully, *authentically* human. One man in particular (who always rejected the label existentialist) embodied such courage.

In January 1960 the French writer and philosopher Albert Camus was killed in a car crash. In his bags were the manuscript of an unfinished autobiographical novel *The First Man* (*Le Premier Homme,* finally published in 1994) and a copy of Nietzsche's *The Joyful Science* (*Die fröhliche Wissenschaft*). The latter was an apposite book. No one has better celebrated the positive, humanist sides of Nietzsche's thought, often seen as inhuman or nihilistic, than Camus.

Most existentialists followed Camus in *living* what they preached, even when this led to unpopularity or danger. In this they followed another of Nietzsche's rousing precepts: Live dangerously! This phrase, like many of Nietzsche's all too catchy aphorisms, is frequently misunderstood and taken at its most superficial. Nietzsche in fact propounded a philosophy so radical that it only began to be appreciated well after his mental collapse in 1889. His collapse, whatever its exact physiological cause, seems almost inevitable for a man who likened himself to an intellectual tight-rope walker suspended perilously above the abyss, daring to look down into the depths of human nature. 'It is not the heights but the depths that are terrible!' he warned, foreseeing the potential terrors of a world where God is dead. But Nietzsche was not the sole or first father of existentialism, whose roots stretch further back in Western thought.

The precursors: 1, Blaise Pascal (1623–62)

'The eternal silence of infinite space terrifies me.' In these words from his *Pensées* ('Thoughts') Pascal voiced the first existential *Angst* (dread, anxiety). A mathematician, scientist and theologian of genius if not a formal philosopher, Pascal was among the few people of his age to appreciate the full significance of the heliocentric system newly revealed by Galileo. In place of the harmonious cosmos revered by pagans and Christians alike, where the music of the celestial spheres leads souls up towards God, Pascal realized that humanity lived on a rock spinning in a silent void. In such a desolate universe, religion could only be a desperate gamble or 'leap of faith', as Kierkegaard later put it.

Insight

The German word *Angst* (*angoisse* in French) has passed into common usage in English. It usually means a general sense of anxiety, anguish or remorse. For existentialists, following Kierkegaard, it means a recurrent state of disquiet or dread caused by human awareness that our future is not predetermined (by God, society or anything else) but must be freely chosen.

Nothing Sartre or other existentialists later wrote surpasses Pascal's pessimism about the human condition. 'The natural misfortune of our mortal and feeble state is so wretched that when we consider it closely, nothing can console us,' he wrote. Instead, we try various forms of escapism, either 'diversions' – politics, social life, gambling – or 'habits', such as the routine of the good citizen with his (or her) family and work. Pascal knew what he was talking about. In his late twenties he inherited enough money to live the life of a gentleman, keeping a coach with six horses (a luxury) and socializing in Paris. His contributions to France's intellectual golden age ranged from mathematics, such as his essay on conic sections *Essai pour les Coniques,* to helping prove the existence of the vacuum. In this latter point he contradicted both the ancient philosopher Aristotle, who had written that 'nature abhors a vacuum', and Descartes himself. Beneath his worldly successes, however, religious anxieties were growing.

On the night of 23 November 1654, while recovering from a severe illness, Pascal had a mystical vision. He recorded it on a scrap of paper he later sewed into the lining of his coat and which was only found after his death. 'Fire! Not the God of the philosophers or scholars, but the God of Abraham, Isaac and Jacob!' he wrote. He now rejected rational theology, indeed reason itself, devoting his life to the mystical asceticism of the Jansenists of Port-Royal, which was sharply at odds with mainstream Catholicism. After another near-death experience, fainting away after his coach almost fell into the Seine, he had a negative epiphany. In it he discovered *le néant*, 'Nothingness', the horrific void beyond life waiting for us all.

At that time newly-invented microscopes and telescopes were revealing the universe at its tiniest and its vastest, expanding endlessly outwards and inwards. Pascal realized that humanity is born midway between Nothingness and the Infinite. 'For what is man in nature? Nothing in relation to infinity, all in relation to nothing, a central point between nothing and all, infinitely far from understanding either... He is equally incapable of seeing the nothingness out of which he was drawn and the infinite in which he is engulfed,' he wrote in *Pensées*.

Pascal's heterodox views remained almost unknown until the nineteenth century. When discovered, they influenced many French writers: Charles Baudelaire (1821–67), often called the 'first modern poet' on whom Sartre wrote some of his most perceptive criticism; the idealist philosopher Henri Bergson (1859–1941) who had enormous influence on many French thinkers; and the existentialists. To many, Pascal was the very first existentialist, three centuries ahead of his true age.

Founding fathers: 1, Søren Kierkegaard (1813–55)

Kierkegaard is Denmark's greatest philosopher and a key figure in the genesis of existentialism. He was also a theologian, psychologist, literary critic and rebel who lived his philosophy with self-destroying ascetic passion. Born in Copenhagen, his youth was scarred by the death of his mother and five of his siblings. He was brought up by an intensely religious father, guilt-ridden because he had once cursed God. Kierkegaard inherited his father's melancholy and guilt, once writing: 'Christianity is suffering'. But he also inherited enough money later to live independently. Studying at Copenhagen University, he encountered Hegelianism, the idealist school of philosophy then dominant across northern Europe. (Denmark was still almost an intellectual province of Germany.)

G.W.F. Hegel (1770–1831) had erected a system so overwhelmingly complete that it seemed to his many admirers literally the last word in philosophy. Human destiny or History, Hegel thought, progresses **dialectically** i.e. by repeated thesis and antithesis, resulting in ever higher syntheses. Finally, History reaches the Absolute, where *Geist* (spirit/mind, a resonant word in German with no real English equivalent) attains full self-awareness. 'History', declared Hegel, 'is the cyclical manifestation of the progressive embodiment of the *Geist*.' For Hegel, here following the mainstream of both Christian and pagan Western thought, the universe is intelligible because it is fundamentally rational. 'The real is the rational and the rational is real,' he wrote. He came to see the authoritarian if efficient Prussian state of his day as currently embodying the Absolute. Hegel also saw philosophy as encompassing religion. He considered all religion as primitively symbolic, despite being ostensibly Christian himself.

Kierkegaard had a mystical experience in 1838 that filled him with 'indescribable joy'. It helped him to reject completely Hegel's grand abstract schema, for it made the individual a mere cog in the machine of historical progress, deprived of all responsibility. He took as his role model Socrates (469–399 BCE), the Greek philosopher noted for his intellectual independence and utter disregard for worldly repute and success – indeed for life, for he was the one Greek thinker executed for his ideas. Kierkegaard wrote his thesis on this founder of the philosophical awkward squad who had *lived*, not just thought, his philosophy.

Insight

Kierkegaard, like many philosophers and artists, questioned the idea of progress in general, not because it makes people miserable but because it could make life too comfortable. Technical progress promises – threatens – endless further distractions from the real existential questions of life, which are at heart religious and philosophical. He would have loathed television and the internet.

Socrates had compared himself to a gadfly, stinging fellow Athenians out of their complacent ignorance in his search for an answer to the question: 'How should we live?' Socrates never found an answer to this, claiming only to be a 'midwife' to truth – unlike Hegel, who claimed knowledge of the whole of reality. Central to Socrates' philosophy (notably in *Symposium* and *Phaedrus*) is the analogy between intellectual and erotic passion. The love of truth springs ultimately from the same desire as the love of beauty in an individual.

Kierkegaard's Christian version of Socrates' quest for truth involved similar use of irony, parody and satire. While not fatal, this path made him similarly unpopular, costing him friends such as the writer Hans Christian Andersen, public respect – he was mocked for his odd appearance as well as his heterodox views – and his fiancée Regine. But, as a youthful letter (31 August 1835) reveals, he was determined to seek the truth: 'The thing is to understand myself, to see what God really wishes me to do: the thing is to find a truth which is true for me, to find the idea for which I can live and die...'

Kierkegaard's impassioned Christianity recalls Pascal's in its rejection of easy, comforting, *reasonable* religion. Advocating a 'crucifixion of reason', he attacked the flaccid Danish Lutheranism of his day as strongly as he did Hegelianism. Typical of the complacency he loathed was a funeral address given in 1854 by Hans Martensen, a bishop (and Hegelian), eulogizing another bishop as one of the greatest Christians since the Apostles. Such sanctimonious waffle struck Kierkegaard as intolerable. He saw Christianity not as reiterating church dogma but as requiring from every believer the need to make existential choices that will decide their eternal salvation or damnation. The pressure of such choices creates existential anxiety or dread (Angst).

Kierkegaard explored this theme in several short books written under various pseudonyms, some more plausible than others (Johannes de Silentio, Hilarius Bogbinder, Climacus): *Either/Or* and *Fear and Trembling* (both 1843); *The Concept of Anxiety* (1844); *Stages on Life's Way* (1845); and *Sickness Unto Death* (1849). He outlined how the Christian must move from the attitude of the aesthete, who pursues life's pleasures with elegant intelligence but avoids any commitments, via the ethical standpoint of someone who accepts social obligations but ultimately finds life without God worthless, to the religious person, ready to make any sacrifice for God.

The sacrifice Kierkegaard focused on in *Fear and Trembling*, his most vivid book, was that by Abraham, the Jewish patriarch, of his only son Isaac. An ethical hero such as Socrates had to sacrifice his life for the sake of universal ethical laws, but Abraham had to break the most fundamental ethical law to obey an omnipotent God's command. (He did not actually have to sacrifice Isaac, it turned out, as God intervened in the form of an angel who presented a ram instead.) Kierkegaard termed Abraham's act the 'teleological suspension of the ethical'. It transgressed morality to reach a higher end (*telos*) beyond ethics. Yet 'Faith's Knight', as Kierkegaard called Abraham, could not tell at the time he drew his knife whether he really was obeying God. He had to make his choice in a 'leap of faith', a phrase that encapsulates Kierkegaard's whole philosophy.

In *Concluding Unscientific Postscript* (1846) Kierkegaard attacked the idea that faith can ever be the outcome of objective reasoning. Faith leaves no room for debate, for it is the result of an individual's subjective passion, unmediated by church or dogma. Believers must reject any rational support for their faith 'to permit the absurd to stand out in all its clarity, in order that the individual may believe it if he wills it.' Only through faith can individuals discover their authentic selves, and so be judged by God.

'If there were no eternal consciousness in man, if at the bottom of everything there were only a wild ferment, a power that in dark passions produced everything great or inconsequential; if an unfathomable insatiable emptiness lay hid beneath everything, what would life be but despair?' Kierkegaard demanded (*Fear and Trembling*). His ultra-Protestant answer to this question – faith against all odds – had less influence on Christians, reluctant to accept that Christianity is 'infinitely improbable', even *absurd,* than on twentieth-century atheists. Existentialists such as Karl Jaspers and Heidegger in Germany and Sartre in France accepted Kierkegaard's demand that, to live authentically, individuals must reject popular opinion and take control of their destiny by a blind leap beyond reason.

Kierkegaard and *Don Giovanni*

'In a way I can say of *Don Giovanni* what Donna Elvira says to him: "You murderer of my happiness." This work has so diabolically enraptured me that I can never forget it. It has driven me, like Elvira, out of the calm night of the cloister.' So wrote Kierkegaard in his *Journal* of 1839, an odd statement from such a puritanical thinker. *Don Giovanni* is Mozart's opera of 1787 about the mythical superstud Don Juan, who cheats, kills and sleeps his way around Europe – his manservant Leporello lists more than a thousand women the Don has seduced. Yet bizzarely, the philosopher's passion for Mozart's music was as great as Nietzsche's for Wagner's. In a section of *Either/Or*, entitled 'The Musical Erotic', Kierkegaard declared that music is the art that best expresses sensuality because it is the most abstract of arts. Like language, it unfolds in time not space, but language expresses the spirit while music conveys sensuality.

Kierkegaard claimed that Christianity had encouraged both great music and true sensuality by contrasting the spirit with the flesh. To Kierkegaard, the Catholic Middle Ages had promulgated endless war between the spirit and the flesh, a conflict first introduced to humanity by Christianity. Each of the polar opposites in this cosmic battle was personified in one character, the representative of the flesh being Don Juan. 'Don Juan... is the incarnation of the flesh, or the inspiration of the flesh by the spirit of the flesh itself.'

Kierkegaard described the varied stages of erotic pursuit by taking characters from Mozart's greatest operas. The first sensual awakening, diffused and wistful, is embodied in Cherubino, the page from *The Marriage of Figaro* who does not love any one person, merely the idea of love. In *The Magic Flute* Papageno cheerfully seeks and finds his mate Papagena. But the real erotic avatar is Don Giovanni, who incarnates erotic energy. Kierkegaard saw in Don Giovanni not a particular individual but a 'power of nature, the demonic, which as little tires of seducing as the wind tires of raging or the sea of surging.' The superhuman energy of his desire animates and controls the other characters in the opera, who are mere puppets of his will (except for the Commander, who stands outside the main action). Music is supremely suited to express the urgency of erotic desire because in music uniquely form and content are one.

The precursors: 2, Fyodor Dostoyevsky (1821–81)

Fyodor Dostoyevsky, one of the greatest Russian novelists, is also renowned as a leading precursor of twentieth-century existentialism, principally for *Notes from Underground*. The scholar Walter Kaufmann called this slim book the 'best overture for existentialism ever written'. It was an overture rooted in bitter personal experience.

In 1849 Dostoyevsky, then a young idealistic liberal, was unjustly sentenced to death for alleged involvement in a conspiracy. Led out to the scaffold with others, he heard his death sentence read out. Twenty minutes later his reprieve was announced. But in those 20 minutes, while a priest went up to each of the condemned with a cross, he felt he was living through infinite time. 'Nothing was so dreadful at that time as the continual thought, "What if I were not to die! What if I could go back to life – what eternity! It would all be mine. I would turn every minute into an age... I would not waste one!" ' (So Dostoyevsky later described his feelings in *The Idiot*.) Face to face with death, life itself gained an absolute value. The years of penal servitude in Siberia that followed turned Dostoyevsky into a mystical Slavophil reactionary – a change less paradoxical than it seems in a Russia only superficially Westernized.

In 1864 Dostoyevsky, now free again, published *Notes from Underground*. Its first part consists of one of the most remarkable monologues in literature. In it, the nameless 'Underground Man', a former petty clerk in Russia's vast bureaucracy, moans and rants, venting his resentment against his superiors and all humanity. He starts in typical self-pity: 'I am a sick man... I am an angry man, I am an unattractive man. I think there is something wrong with my liver.' He goes on to compare himself unflatteringly with a beetle: 'I couldn't even become an insect...I have often tried to become an insect but I was incapable even of that... To think too much is an illness.'

Underground Man attacks science, maths, reason and the 'great crystal palace', a reference to the Crystal Palace of London's Great Exhibition in 1851, symbol of technological progress. 'Civilization develops in man nothing but an extra capacity to absorb sensations,' he snarls. There is no action in the book, no other character, giving it the hellish claustrophobia of Sartre's play *No Exit (Huis Clos)*. The book is finally an experiment in self-exposure, Dostoyevsky's 'most utterly naked pages', as a critic said.

He never wrote anything so openly existentialist again. But in the masterpieces of his maturity – *Crime and Punishment, The Idiot, The Brothers Karamazov, The Devils* – he explored themes that would occupy the twentieth century's finest minds. In *Crime and Punishment* Raskolnikov, an impoverished student disgusted by society, works out a proto-Nietzschean amoral code that permits him to kill a wretched old woman for her money. (Money from the crime will let him continue his studies.) Raskolnikov, however, subsequently succumbs to pity for others. This undoes him as a superman and he finally confesses all to the police.

In *The Brothers Karamazov* Ivan Karamazov, the intellectual of the siblings, tells a parable, *The Grand Inquisitor*, about Christ's return to earth in medieval Seville. Arrested and condemned to death by the Inquisition, Christ is visited in prison by the Grand Inquisitor Torquemada. The ensuing conversation – intended as a refutation of atheism, with the Inquisitor cast as an evil totalitarian – turns into a searching debate on human responsibility and freedom. The Inquisitor, sounding almost philanthropic in his atheism, argues that literally following Christ's way will lead to religious and social chaos; far better to accept the dogma of the Catholic church, which keeps humanity in happy, servile ignorance. Christ replies only by kissing the Inquisitor on his 'bloodless aged lips', quashing all arguments. He is finally freed on condition that he preaches no more. Later in the book the mystical Father Zossima offers a more cogent defence of Christianity and Ivan has a feverish vision of the Devil who, to his disgust, turns out to be a thoroughly vulgar figure.

Dostoyevsky's beliefs – not only in the Russian Orthodox church (which entailed hostility to most things Western) but even in the autocratic Tsarist regime – might make him an unlikely ancestor of existentialism. Yet as the first writer to delve so deep into the human psyche, he raised many questions that were later taken up by the existentialists. Nietzsche called Dostoyevsky 'the only psychologist from whom I have learned something'.

Insight

Whether Christ or Torquemada has won the argument in *The Brothers Karamazov* is left to the reader to decide – an existentialist choice. We should beware of attributing to authors opinions expressed by their characters in any work of fiction, especially those as toweringly polyphonic as Dostoyevsky's novels.

Founding fathers: 2, Friedrich Nietzsche (1844–1900)

In January 1889 a retired German professor whose writings were still mostly unknown collapsed in the streets of Turin. He probably had tertiary syphilis. Certainly he had just started an earthquake of unparalleled magnitude in Western philosophy, as he realized. Its after-shocks are still being registered. Friedrich Nietzsche is among the handful of genuinely revolutionary thinkers. He is also among the most quotable and so misquoted. No quotation is more famous than his declaration: 'God is dead!' Often forgotten is the follow-up: 'Now we want the **Übermensch** (superman) to live!' Nietzsche was an atheist but one of a peculiarly joyful sort. He was also a psychologist of astonishing acuity and a moralist unafraid to face the full consequences of the death of God.

Nietzsche came from a deeply clerical dynasty – his father and *both* his grandfathers had been Lutheran pastors. As a child he played at being a clergyman so often that he was nicknamed 'little pastor'. This gave his adult atheism an explosively personal quality, tantamount to religious conviction, missing in most earlier philosophers. Epicurus

(341–270 BCE), for example, had been an atheist but a discreet one. The gods, he said tactfully, exist but live infinitely far from us, unconcerned with humanity. Voltaire (1694–1778), supposedly a deist but really a closet atheist, had had to express his views obliquely in satire, for example when writing about the Lisbon earthquake of 1755 in *Candide*. (This catastrophe had killed tens of thousands of the devout worshipping in church, undermining belief in an omnipotent, benevolent God.) Voltaire's tirades against Christianity were mere squibs compared with Nietzsche's elemental assault, however.

Long study of the pagan Graeco-Roman world had already led Nietzsche to reject his childhood faith by 1865. That year he came across *The World as Will and Representation* (*Die Welt als Wille und Vorstellung*) by Arthur Schopenhauer (1788–1860). Overwhelmed by this 'dismal dynamic genius', as he called the man he always revered as his educator, he adopted Schopenhauer's pessimistic, godless cosmogony. This, roughly following the schema of Immanuel Kant (1724–1804), divided the universe into the *noumenal*, an unknowable, undivided, brutal and amoral 'Will' or reality beyond human consciousness, and the *phenomenal*, the multiple daily world we know. Schopenhauer's bleak view of the phenomenal world as a place of unmitigated suffering led him to advocate asceticism and compassion – qualities notably absent from his own life – to transcend it. Art, especially classical music, could offer a discerning few another escape.

Nietzsche's first great work *The Birth of Tragedy* (*Die Gerburt der Tragödie*, 1872), shows little trace of pessimism, however. It is a lyrical, intoxicated celebration of Dionysus, Greek god of drama, wine and passion. Nietzsche was the first to realize the irrational god's importance to the Greeks. Like Schopenhauer, he accorded art a central role in human life. 'Only if viewed aesthetically can the world be justified,' he declared, but he was not espousing an escapist art-for-art's-sake stance. 'How much the Greeks must have suffered to be so beautiful!' he continued, realizing that the Greeks' high culture arose from their overcoming their very hard lives. His own elation stemmed partly from his relationship with the composer Richard Wagner (1813–83), another Schopenhauer admirer whose music had fascinated Nietzsche since he had first heard it. 'It thrills every nerve, every fibre in my being,' he wrote in 1868. The two geniuses were mutually inspiring friends until, disgusted by what he saw as the composer's sell-out to the new imperial Germany, Nietzsche became Wagner's most savage critic. Even more significantly, he rejected Schopenhauer's pessimism and 'metaphysics'.

In a succession of books he attacked the deep-rooted metaphysical bias of Western thought, claiming that only this physical phenomenal world is real. In *Human, All Too Human* (*Menschliches, Allzumenschliches*), published in 1878 on the centenary of Voltaire's death and subtitled *A Book for Free Spirits*, he sounded an almost scientific note. With *Daybreak* (*Morgenröte* 1881) he began his war against Christian morality: 'Christianity has succeeded in making Eros and Aphrodite – great ennobling ideals – into goblins and phantoms... We have to learn to think differently, to feel differently.'

In *The Joyful Science* (*Die fröhliche Wissenschaft*, 1882), he openly proclaimed the death of God:

Have you not heard of the madman who lit a lantern in the bright morning, ran to the market-place and cried incessantly: 'I am looking for God! I am looking for God!' This invokes mockery from bystanders. 'Have you lost him then?' said one. 'Did he lose his way like a child?' But their laughter dies as the madman pierces them with his glance. 'Where has God gone?' he cried. 'I shall tell you. We have killed him – you and I. We are all his murderers. But how have we done this?... Who gave us the sponge to wipe away the entire horizon? What did we do when we unchained this earth from its sun? Where is it orbiting? Where are we orbiting? Away from all suns?... Aren't we drifting through empty nothing? Has it not grown colder? Is not endless night closing in on us?'

This voices true existentialist *Angst*. We are alone, leading meaningless lives in a godless universe. Pascal and Kierkegaard had also felt such icy winds around them but, while rejecting reason, they had embraced their own versions of Christianity. In his quest for truth, Nietzsche rejected both Christianity and rationalism *without becoming nihilistic*. He thought true nihilists were those who, without a real belief in God, still clung to the ethics of a 'putrefying' deity. In place of this feeble post-Christian ethos, Nietzsche announced the coming of the Übermensch, the Superman, in *Thus Spoke Zarathustra* (*Also Sprach Zarathustra* 1883–5).

Insight

Nietzsche particularly despised those critics and thinkers who tried to create a form of secularized, liberal Christianity, accusing them in effect of **bad faith**. Among them he placed the German scholar David Strauss (1808–74), who tried to interpret the Bible historically, and George Eliot (1819–80), the English novelist influenced by Strauss, who abandoned her childhood Christianity but tried to retain its ethical teaching.

'Behold, I am the prophet of the lightning... this lightning is called the Übermensch... All gods are dead. Now we want the Übermensch to live!' By Übermensch Nietzsche meant not a racially superior or genetically modified type but an intellectually, morally and aesthetically higher being. 'What is the ape to humanity? A laughing stock, a painful embarrassment. Just so shall humanity be to the Übermensch... Behold I teach you the Übermensch. The Übermensch is the meaning of the earth.' To counter any undue exuberance this might induce, he propounded the idea of Eternal Recurrence, of everything forever returning. With it came the injunction of *amor fati*, the love of (one's own) fate. The Übermensch must say Yes to life's pains as much as to its joys, again and again and again. Not an easy option.

In *The Genealogy of Morals* (*Zur Genealogie der Moral*, 1887), often thought his subtlest work, Nietzsche intensified his attack on Judaeo-Christianity, claiming that even its highest morals were essentially base. Christianity poses as a religion of love, but this love stems from fear and *ressentiment* (resentment, envy).

According to Nietzsche, ancient aristocrats had called the qualities they naturally valued – bravery, intelligence, nobility, beauty – 'good'. Qualities valued by their slaves – humility, mass solidarity, charity – were simply 'bad'. Judaeo-Christianity, at first a religion of martyrs, slaves and the oppressed, had inverted the old morality. With Christianity's triumph, a 'reversal of values' made **slave morality** dominant, giving voice to the *ressentiment* of those 'who, powerless in this world, compensate by an imagined revenge in the next.'

The 'incredible revenge' of slaves upon their masters was assisted by Plato and Socrates, who had earlier undermined the heroic values derived from Homer (*c.*750 BCE), first and greatest of Greek poets. 'Christianity is Platonism for the masses,' Nietzsche wrote, meaning that Platonism and Christianity devalued humanity's healthy instincts (and also that the masses cannot do philosophy). Nietzsche called for a counter-reversal of values. This would permit aristocratic free spirits to flourish and humanity again to enjoy life on earth, free from needless guilt about innate sexual and social urges.

Perhaps Nietzsche was half-right. Almost no one can live all the time following the self-sacrificing precepts of Christ's Sermon on the Mount (or the Buddhist equivalent, the *Dhammapada*). We make ourselves neurotically guilty, even ill, trying to do so. Better to acknowledge our real instincts – the instincts of life itself – and plan our morals accordingly. Yet Nietzsche's radical ethical ideas still appear brutal. Schopenhauer, in ousting the deity, had seen no need for revolutionary changes in morality. Nor have many later atheists. Bertrand Russell's renowned atheism hardly affected his liberal ethics – he can sound much like a woolly old liberal. Compared to Nietzsche, Richard Dawkins' loud attacks on Christianity seem merely the spluttering of an irascible Oxford don on television. Nietzsche alone had the vision and courage to realize – and accept – all that the death of God entailed: 'an overturning of the tables of the law'. Although not every existentialist was an atheist, all are Nietzsche's children, forced to re-examine, perhaps reject, every aspect of morality.

The nihilist existentialist Emil Cioran (1911–95)

Not all existentialists said 'Yes!' or even 'Yes, but…' to life. One firmly said 'No!' Emil Cioran was among the brilliant twentieth-century Romanian artists and intellectuals who settled in Paris. Unlike the sculptor Constantin Brancusi and the playwright Eugène Ionesco, compatriots who became world-famous, Cioran remained little known, living in poverty. This was partly due to personal preference – he was uninterested in fame, whether in life or after death – and partly to his radical pessimism. While Nietzsche exulted in life and Camus tried to reconcile human nobility with cosmic absurdity, Cioran accepted the futility and insignificance of **existence**. He wrote: 'Although I feel that my tragedy is the greatest in history, greater than the fall of empires, I am aware of my total insignificance. I am totally convinced that I count for nothing in this universe, yet I feel that mine is the only real existence. If forced to choose between the world and myself, I would reject the world, its light and laws, unafraid to glide alone in absolute nothingness. Although my life is a torture, I cannot renounce it because I do not believe in any absolute values for which I could sacrifice myself' (*On the Heights of Despair*, p. 33). Cioran welcomed his many illnesses almost like a Christian saint: 'Only sickness gives birth to serious and deep values. Whatever is not born out of sickness has merely an aesthetic value… Genuine illness links us to metaphysical realities the healthy man cannot understand.'

Cioran was no saint, however. Going further even than Dostoyevsky's most repellent characters, he preached an amoral subjectivism. 'Who can precisely say that my neighbour suffers more than I do, or that Jesus suffered more than all of us? … Each person remains with his own suffering, which he thinks absolute and limitless… Each subjective existence is absolute to itself. For this reason each man lives as if he were the centre of the universe or of history' (*On the Heights of Despair*, p. 33). Surpassing Sartre,

(Contd)

who famously declared 'Hell is other people', Cioran declared that 'we are here to make other people miserable' and admitted that, if he could, he would 'blow up the world.'

Cioran's pessimism recalls that of Arthur Schopenhauer (1788–1860), an important influence on his thinking. While not advocating ascetic self-denial like Schopenhauer, Cioran shared the German philosopher's faith in the redemptive power of classical music. 'Bach's music is the only argument proving the creation of the Universe cannot be regarded as a complete failure', he told *Newsweek* magazine (4 December 1989). Cioran, the philosopher of despair, sickness and decay, retained a latent religious streak that led him to search for a meaning to life while almost certain that his quest was hopeless. This makes him an existentialist of an extreme yet authentic type.

The precursors: 3, Franz Kafka (1883–1924)

If the concept of being born or 'thrown' into a particular time and place is accepted by all existentialists, few have awoken one day to find themselves transformed into a giant insect. This, however, is the fate of Gregor Samsa, protagonist of *Metamorphosis* (*Die Verwandlung*), a novella Kafka published in 1915. Bewildered by the change, alienated from everyone and racked by guilt that he can no longer work to support his family, Gregor ends up being abused, starved and finally killed by his appalled relatives.

Kafka is among the select few writers who have given their name to an adjective, in his case *kafkaesque*, meaning nightmarishly bureaucratic and dehumanized. The term aptly describes the experiences of K, protagonist of his two main novels, *The Trial* (*Der Prozess*) and *The Castle* (*Das Schloss*). *The Trial* starts with the chilling sentence: 'Someone must have been telling lies about Josef K, for without having done anything wrong he was arrested one morning.' Josef K is caught up in an unending judicial process whose rules, as arbitrary as they are obscure, are hidden from even its highest officials. Trying to escape, he makes several mistakes that doom him: he trustingly accepts there is a bona fide case against him, he fails to understand the court's arcane rules and he refuses assistance from unknown helpers. Finally, he goes to his execution with odd meekness. Whether this shows brave, existentialist acceptance of fate or spineless, even masochistic acquiescence in his oppression is unclear. Most of Kafka's works are highly ambiguous and all his major novels were left unfinished.

Kafka was born to a Jewish family in Prague, now the Czech capital but then in the vast Austro-Hungarian empire. His father Hermann, a successful businessman, was large, loud and coarse, the writer's exact opposite. Hermann Kafka tended to bully his frail hypersensitive son but he also supported him financially whenever needed. Kafka had a successful career in a state insurance company until tuberculosis forced him to retire. (It finally killed him.) His experience of the tortuous workings of bureaucracy colours his works.

Kafka's native language, in which he always wrote, was German, although he also spoke Czech. He hardly felt Jewish in a religious sense. 'What have I in common with Jews? I have hardly anything in common with myself and should stand very quietly in a corner, content that I can breathe,' he said with typical self-deprecation. He was part of the brilliant early twentieth-century generation of secularized central European Jews, many of whom were later murdered by the Nazis. (Two of Kafka's sisters died in the death camps.) Max Brod (1884–1968), another German–Jewish writer, who met Kafka at Prague University, became his close friend and literary executor. Moving in Prague's German-speaking literary elite, Kafka was no recluse. Yet he published relatively little in his lifetime and on his deathbed reputedly asked Brod to burn all his manuscripts. Fortunately, Brod ignored his wishes.

In *The Castle* K, a land surveyor summoned to an obscure nameless village, makes repeated attempts to meet the mysterious ruler Count Westwest or the equally elusive official Klamm, but without success. Endless bureaucratic obstacles prevent K from ever finding the 'gentlemen' in the castle high on its hill.

Insight

In some readings the Castle symbolizes an impossibly remote God that K himself can never reach. According to others the silent Castle – 'hidden, veiled in mist and darkness, without even a glimmer of light to show that the castle was there' – and its absent Count symbolize the death of God. News of this death has not yet reached the villagers below, who still live in awe of the Castle and its laws. Echoes here of Nietzsche's *The Joyful Science*.

Kafka's German is unusually lucid (something not always apparent in translation), but his works are complex allegories or parables laced with black humour. He also wrote four short tales called *Parables*, of which *Couriers* is the last. 'All men, offered the choice of being kings or couriers, like children choose to be couriers. Therefore there are only couriers. They hurry about the world shouting to each other messages that have lost all meaning, since there are no kings. They would like to end their miserable aimless lives but dare not, because they have sworn oaths to serve.' The human condition in a nutshell. Midway between Nietzsche and the existentialists proper, Kafka uncannily anticipated the world into which Heidegger's man (in *Being and Time*) is 'thrown', the godless world of Sartre, the absurd world of Camus.

10 THINGS TO REMEMBER

1 *Existentialism, while seeming new in 1945, had a long intellectual ancestry.*

2 *As much of this ancestry was literary as 'philosophical'.*

3 *Few existentialist ancestors/precursors were ever formal philosophers.*

4 *Some key proto-existentialists (Pascal, Dostoyevsky) were Christians.*

5 *Most of the other existentialists were 'cheerful' atheists.*

6 *Most proto-existentialists lived what they preached, 'living dangerously'.*

7 *Existentialism often entails the demolition of earlier systems of thought.*

8 *Despite the above, existentialism is (almost) never nihilistic.*

9 *Existentialists stress the value of lived, embodied thought.*

10 *The existentialists' concept of being 'thrown into the world' makes them unusually concerned with this world.*

3

Between birth and death

In this chapter you will learn:
- *that Heidegger's 'world' involves personal meaning and significance*
- *that we live forwards, allowing circumstances to provide possibilities*
- *that death is the point at which we see our lives as a whole*

Many of the fundamental ideas and themes that were to shape existentialism appear in Heidegger's *Being and Time*. Published in 1927, it was a hugely influential book.

What Heidegger set out to do was to examine the nature of **'being'**, asking the most general, abstract and fundamental question of all: 'What is it to "be"?' The quest to find an answer to this, which has a long history in philosophy going back at least to Aristotle (384–322 BCE), is generally known as 'ontology'. But where do you start such a quest?

Heidegger realized that the best starting point for a general understanding of 'being' was to consider it from the point of view of the human being; not in an abstract sense, but a person engaged with his or her world living, working, planning and so on. So what he considers is not simply a human individual as might be described by science, 'out there' as an object in the world, but what it is to experience oneself as a human individual, involved at every moment in living in the world.

To do this, he used the term Dasein. A literal translation of this would be 'being there' or 'being here'. He is trying to describe what it is to *be* human.

Insight

Heidegger makes things even more difficult for readers by stringing words together and giving them very specific meanings, often very different from their ordinary use. Being-in-the-world is the experience of engagement with things, having a past, planning a future and so on. It is not the same as 'being in the world' in the sense of existing within the sort of objective world that science describes. Confused? Read on...

To appreciate a little of this, let us look at just two words, which Heidegger uses in very specific ways:

▸ **World:** *We usually think of the world as the collection of everything that exists 'out there'. Heidegger sees it differently. 'The world' for Heidegger (or rather, 'the world' for Dasein – the human being), is more like a structure or framework within which we live. It is where we find meaning and significance. 'My world' is more than a scientific description of the universe a world within which I operate. That kind of 'world' is part of me, just as much as I am part of it. My experience of being human is an experience of having a 'world' of that sort.*

▸ **Time:** *We usually assume time to be a sequence of instantaneous 'nows', rushing towards us from the future and disappearing into the past. But from the standpoint of Dasein (the human being) in his or her 'world', it means something quite different. At any one time, we anticipate what will happen next – we plan, we organize, we hope, we fear. Much of what we do, and how we understand ourselves, is given in terms of that which does not yet exist. But at the same time, who we are today has been determined by what happened in the past. We carry with us, if not a burden, then at least a volume of experience. Hence, for us as we are now, experiencing what*

it is to be human, time shapes what we have become, and what
we wish to be. We are who we are, because we live in time.
We live by what does not exist – a nothingness – either because
it has not yet happened, or because it is already past. This is
something that Sartre was later to develop in his book Being
and Nothingness.

Insight

Heidegger's is a work of **phenomenology** – it is an attempt to
'see' or to 'show' what is the case, rather than using analysis
or logical argument to prove it to be so. It is an exploration of
how we encounter ourselves living in our world.

Dasein is thus not simply a 'subject', separable from the 'objective'
world outside, but is a combination, a being-with of self and
world. *What I am is not separable from the world in which I am.*

Thrownness

We are all born into a set of circumstances, not of our own
choosing. We are 'thrown' (not just at birth, but all the time)
into our world, which we experience as having this quality of
'thrownness' (*Geworfenheit*). I find myself pitched into it, and
within it I have to try to make sense of my life and sort out my
possibilities.

Insight

My circumstances do not determine the choices I make,
they simply provide me with a range of possibilities.

The world revealed by science, however, is objective; it is observed
'out there', separate from my subjective experience. It is a matter
of space, time, physical entities and forces; it appears to be totally
conditioned by physical laws. On the other hand, the world in
which the human person finds himself or herself living is more than
that. It is not just a world of space and time that could be measured

scientifically, but a world of meaning and significance. We move, like a spider, within a web of meanings. Without meaning and direction, without some project, how is one to know what to do, what to choose, what direction to take?

So, if science cannot provide a ready-made sense of meaning, significance or value, we have to set about constructing it for ourselves.

The world in which we find ourselves is one in which we have a particular set of circumstances and therefore a particular set of possibilities. Not everything is open to us – much will depend on our background – but we at least have the freedom to choose which of the possibilities we wish to take.

Goodbye Descartes!

In probably what is the most celebrated conclusion in the history of philosophy, Descartes, determined to reach some point of certainty, realized that (without self-contradiction) he could not doubt the fact of his own thinking. He therefore declared *cogito ergo sum*, 'I think therefore I am'.

And from that famous *cogito* there sprang up the assumption that there was an absolute divide between mind and body – the body physical and extended in space, the mind non-physical. And so, thinking about the way our mind relates to the world, it was assumed that the mind looked out on 'the world' and knew it only through sense perceptions which it processed. That view raised a whole raft of issues. If our minds are non-physical and distinct from our bodies, how can we ever know another person? Do I watch your body, including its actions and its language, and somehow deduce that there is a mind hidden in there somewhere? If mind and body are utterly different, how can my mind produce physical activity just by thinking and choosing to do something? How can my body influence my mind, as when I'm drunk or exhausted?

The mind became (in a caricature of Descartes produced by his twentieth-century critic, Gilbert Ryle) a 'ghost in a machine'. So, from the seventeenth century to the early twentieth, it was assumed that the world was some form of physical mechanism, controlled by its own natural, physical laws, whereas the mind was somehow linked to the body, but never part of the world that we experience.

By contrast, a key feature of existentialism is that the mind makes absolutely no sense if it is removed from its engagement with the world. The mind is involved and active, and that is what gives it character. To use Sartre's famous expression – to which we shall return – 'existence precedes essence', what we are develops out of what we live.

Insight

You, a separate, thinking thing, look out upon the physical world, and are able to make a difference to it, through the actions of your body. That, in crude caricature, is the general sense of Cartesian dualism that the existentialists rejected.

Cartesian dualism placed a huge gulf between the mental life of individuals and the physical world. The danger of such a dualist approach is that each person becomes an isolated thinking centre. In rejecting this, the existentialists wanted to consider human life as it is lived in the world: a life of relationships, a life that is embedded in a particular set of circumstances, a life that is always aware of the process of ageing and of the certainty of death. For Heidegger, we are thrown into the world, engaged with it, and always living forwards.

Key thought

You can only appreciate existentialism once you see the limitations of what it rejected:

▶ *The attempt to see human beings in terms of pure, disembodied thought*
▶ *The assumption that evidence and scientific method could answer all human questions*

How utterly different and revolutionary Heidegger's thought is here. He is not trying to analyse what might be the 'true' self; he is not attempting to analyse how mind relates to body. He is simply helping us to look at what it is to be a human being in our world. Dasein is how I experience myself in my world; indeed, my world is part of Dasein.

Using rather different language, but with the same implications, Merleau-Ponty argues, in *The Phenomenology of Perception*, that thinking is not limited to private states of consciousness, but involves a 'momentum of transcendence which is my very being, the simultaneous contact with my own being and with the world's being' (p. 377, translation by Colin Smith, Routledge, 1962). And here we have the basic fact that the self and the world are inseparable: what we are, what we know of ourselves, is intimately linked to the world in which we are embedded. For Merleau-Ponty, 'love is consciousness of loving, will is consciousness of willing' (p. 378). We are aware of ourselves only as we are aware of our relationship with our world.

Halfway Husserl

The young Martin Heidegger, while studying in a theological seminary in Freiburg during 1909 and 1910 (he was originally thinking of ordination and studied theology, was fascinated by

Logical Investigations by Edmund Husserl. It was this that led him to switch to philosophy and to leave the seminary.

From Heidegger's perspective his teacher, Husserl, provided a first stage of movement away from Descartes and towards his own position. Husserl's philosophy is described as phenomenology. It explores the world as we experience it. It gets away from the dualism of thinking that experience is separate from reality. What we experience is reality itself.

This counters the view of Kant in the eighteenth century, who made an absolute distinction between things-in-themselves (noumena) and things-as-we-perceive-them-to-be (phenomena). For phenomenology the essence of something is not hidden, but is known in its various phenomenal manifestations.

Insight

This is fundamental to existentialism. There are no hidden essences, and that includes you and me. We are what we do; we are what others can see. The 'real' self, which nobody else can understand, is an indulgent fantasy.

But even before he had discovered Husserl, Heidegger had studied Brentano's *On the manifold meaning of being since Aristotle*, written in 1862. Heidegger's reading of this, in 1907, introduced him to the study of 'being' (ontology) which was to be the main thrust of his early work. He was reluctant to be seen as an existentialist in the 1940s because his own quest was broader, and his use of human existence was really just a means to his end of understanding 'being'.

But Brentano and Husserl introduced to him another feature of human thought: intentionality, the view that consciousness is always directed towards something. If we hope, or love, or fear, we always do that with reference to some object – we hope 'for' something, we 'will' something to happen. In other words our experience takes on what was to be called an 'intentional stance'. We are aware of ourselves as selves, but always in relation to something else; we are selves within a world, an experienced world to which our mental states are constantly related.

Insight

This suggests that we always experience things 'as' something. What we encounter is not just bits of raw data, but an object which we immediately relate to ourselves.

However, Heidegger was never satisfied with Husserl's work. In focusing on the phenomena of experience, Husserl leaves aside ('brackets out') the question of whether we can know if *what* we experience corresponds to some external thing *that* we experience. In other words, to rather over-simplify the matter, Husserl is still about what happens in the head and sense organs – his phenomena are about *our experience*. And this, for him, was important, because it enabled him to shed metaphysical questions and just concentrate on our own experiences, a process that he felt gave his philosophy a scientific credibility. It was a matter of observation and description, rather than speculation, and that was crucial to the phenomenological approach.

But Heidegger felt that Husserl had not yet properly broken free from the tendency that Descartes had promoted – namely to see the subject self as set apart from the external, objective world. Husserl had come halfway with his phenomenology. In other words, whereas Husserl had seen the necessity of building up the world on the basis of the phenomena that we experience, Heidegger wants to start with the fact that we are in the world, and all our dealings with it are instrumental.

Insight

In ordinary life we do not stop to question whether the thing in front of us actually exists, we just pick it up and use it – or get out of its way before it eats us, depending on the circumstances!

In Heidegger's view, Husserl still saw thinkers as essentially spectators – looking out at the world of phenomena – and as taking an intentional stance towards that world. For Heidegger you need to get away from this external spectator. He wanted to start from an awareness of the self and the world working together as almost a single entity (in other words, where the self is fully integrated into its world).

Insight

Heidegger does not start by looking at an external, objective world from the standpoint of an internal, subjective self. He starts with the practical world in which we are engaged. The philosophical, metaphysical, scientific world as derived from it and very much secondary to it.

Heidegger therefore felt that it was his task to set aside the whole philosophical tradition from Aristotle through to Husserl, and to start again. In doing so, however, he inevitably built on what had gone before.

Existentialism logically follows from phenomenology, because we philosophize on what we experience, not on what is 'out there' independent of us. But Husserl could still be understood as having a 'personal theatre' view of experience (i.e. going on inside the head and dubiously related to the world 'out there'). Heidegger shifts away from this. The things we experience are there as the given factual reality of our lives.

Existentialism rejects the 'view from nowhere' idea that science should, in theory, offer information that is not influenced by our own perception (a view which is, of course, challenged by many scientists). In practice, the existentialists sought the very opposite – *the view from where I am*, thrown into life in my particular time and place, challenged to make sense of it. We are always engaged.

There is another way of putting this, expressed succinctly by Maurice Merleau-Ponty in the preface to his *Phenomenology of Perception* (1945, English translation by Colin Smith, 1962; p. xvi). He says:

We must not, therefore, wonder whether we really perceive a world, we must instead say: the world is what we perceive.

This is central to existentialism. If you start to question whether what we perceive is the 'actual' world, then you start to make a distinction between the world and the perceiving self that leads straight back to Descartes. For existentialism, what the self experiences is its world. The world is where we are and what we do, it is not detachable.

Heidegger and existentialism

Heidegger did not see himself as an existentialist. His concern was ontology – the study of being – an approach to philosophy he considered to be broader than existentialism. But in working on an ontological analysis of Dasein, he raised many of the issues that characterize existentialism: nothingness, **authenticity**, conscience, guilt, angst, death and so on.

It is also clear that his work had a considerable influence on that of Sartre. Sartre, while held captive in a prisoner-of-war camp, studied Heidegger's *Being and Time* and drafted his own *Being and Nothingness*. His language (e.g. the 'in-itself', as opposed to the 'for-itself') reflects distinctions made by Heidegger. It is therefore probably fair to say that Heidegger has been hugely influential in the development of existential philosophy, without himself being an existentialist.

Karl Jaspers, commenting on *Being and Time,* did not think that represented the right way to do philosophy, since its aim was to help to frame an understanding of Being as a whole, whereas – from Jaspers' existential viewpoint – the task of philosophy should be to concentrate on the individual in his or her situation. Of course, *Being and Time* does consider the individual – after all, it is as individuals that we experience our 'thrownness' and look towards our future – but the key thing to remember is that, for Heidegger, these are simply ways of exploring Dasein.

(Contd)

Heidegger, like Nietzsche, sees true philosophy as emerging out of the failure of conventional reason. Although he provided much of the language and conceptual structures of existential thought, Heidegger's approach was rather different from the radical existentialism of Paris in the 1940s.

As well as influencing Heidegger, Husserl's work also gave a jolt to the reflections of the young Sartre, who suddenly realized that philosophy could be done in direct engagement with the world, rather than in some other abstract world of speculation. He saw also that consciousness was not a private experience, but was a way of being related to the world.

Insight
Existentialism promised to be a philosophy of direct engagement with the world; that is what fired the young Sartre, and that is its ongoing appeal.

Ready-to-hand

Heidegger believed that human existence (Dasein) only made sense in terms of its engagement with its world. We have already looked at two aspects of this – that we are 'thrown' into life, and that we live forwards. In other words, everything we do in the present moment is informed by our past, and everything aims at our future, expressing our hopes, fears, intentions, plans and so on.

Thus, for example, I can pick up a hammer and use it for hammering (to use one of Heidegger's examples). I use it as a tool to achieve what I want. I have an intention, and the hammer becomes a way of achieving it. But the hammer is not a hammer unless I see and use it as such. Encountering it as a hammer is already to declare my relationship to it – for me it is a tool. We thus encounter things in the world *as tools that we can use to achieve our purpose*; Heidegger describes such things as being ready-to-hand (*zuhanden*).

Now this raises a crucial distinction between his approach and the way in which much philosophy looks at 'the world'. We tend to assume that the primary way in which we can understand the world is through science. In other words, we seek for an objective way to measure and understand what is 'out there' to be examined. We think that science reveals the 'real' world, whereas our own particular points of view represent only a personal interpretation.

But Heidegger is suggesting that our prime way of engaging with the world is not a detached, scientific one at all; it is the engaged one of using things that are ready-to-hand. That's not just a tree, it is potentially the wood I need for crafting something; or perhaps it's a patch of shade I need in the garden; or perhaps it will yield a crop of apples. I am not engaged with the tree in the way that a professional arboriculturist would examine it; for me it is something which has a place in 'my world' because it has significance for me.

In *Being and Time* Heidegger uses the example of a pen that won't work. We examine its parts to see what's wrong. That action is to see it as 'present-to-hand' (i.e. as a 'thing' to be observed) but it only happens because it isn't working. If it worked, we'd see it as 'ready-to-hand' and just get on with writing.

Insight

In other words, scientific analysis – seeing things in an objective, detached way – is not our primary way of dealing with the world.

Take an obvious example. If we were to challenge and question everything that we experienced, we might conclude that we really know nothing of the mind of another person, since, following Descartes, the mind is not part of the physical world and therefore not observable. But how could we ever make sense of our life on that basis? We do not, in fact, wait until we can conclude that other people exist before we relate to them! We deal with them first, and only subsequently (if they are behaving very strangely) do we stop and ask whether they have a mind, and if so, whether we can know anything of it. Existentialism starts with the obvious facts of human life and explores their possibilities, threats and responsibilities. It does not stand back from life and try to pull it apart like a scientist examining an unusual specimen.

Interpreting our world

The philosophical term for the study of the way in which we come to interpret and understand something is **Hermeneutics**, and with it comes a traditional problem called the 'hermeneutic circle'. Put simply, this claims that you can't properly understand the parts of something without understanding the whole (after all, we can't even see them as parts unless we recognize that they are parts of something), but at the same time, we can't understand the whole without the parts (because the whole is simply the sum of those parts, and without them, it cannot be perceived). So how can you understand anything?

Insight
In order to look for something, you have to know what it is, otherwise you'd never know if you'd found it! Whatever we understand, we understand *in context*, otherwise we'd never have had any reason to *want* to understand it. Words make sense in the context of sentences.

In *Being and Time* (in what is known as his 'hermeneutic turn') Heidegger argues that we always interpret the world in the context in which we find ourselves – as a student, or as a family person, for example. As our projects and needs change, so do our interpretations. How you interpret your world depends on your activity within it.

Sartre too thinks that the only world we can know stems from the way in which we come to know it. It is shot through with our own ideas and perspectives. This is very different from the scientific view of the world, which attempts to eliminate the human perspective. Science can give 'objective' facts, but is always limited in what it can show. It cannot give a sense of the whole – only the relationship between parts.

Insight

If you discover one fact after another, you end up with a heap of facts. You do not have an overall view of the world, or an interpretation. An interpretation is what makes an account of those facts possible in the first place.

What we can't do is show how the world of our perspectives compares to the 'real' world that is somehow beyond them, for the exact reason that we cannot get *beyond* those perspectives. They are the whole thing for us. The very idea that there is somehow a real world out there, separate from the world we encounter in our experience, is to fall straight back into Cartesian dualism. The real world is the one I encounter, the one in which I act, the one in which I find tools ready-to-hand.

We are, of course, always in a particular set of circumstances, and we cannot pretend it can be otherwise, but our knowledge of the world is also the knowledge of our own *possibilities*, in other words it is future orientated. We are not just seeing what is there, we are seeing what is there *for us*, what we can use, what we shall choose. Existential interpretation is never detached from the experience of being engaged in the world.

Death

Wittgenstein famously declared that death is not an event in life. And that, of course, is perfectly true, since we never live to experience our own death. Wittgenstein's statement does no more than reflect the ancient Greek philosophy of Epicurus (341–270 BCE), who saw death as the cessation of experience and therefore nothing to be feared, since without sensation there could be no pain.

But when Heidegger comes to examine death, he means by it something quite different. Death is certain, but its circumstances are unknown to us. It is therefore understandable that many people push the idea of death away – it is something that happens to other people, and that will happen to me one day, but not just yet.

We cannot understand death by seeing the death of others, for that is only a matter of experiencing our loss of them, or their ceasing to be in our world, or of their radical failure to become what they might have become had they lived longer. But we cannot experience what they experience. We can only really appreciate what death means by confronting our own death. Death is what makes you, finally, the person you are. Heidegger's basic question is, therefore: What meaning does my life have in the light of my death?

One thing is clear: in Heidegger's analysis, we always live forwards – our lives are always incomplete, waiting, planning, searching, fearing, hoping for the next thing to happen. The fact is, we never normally see our lives 'as a whole', as something complete. They are always open ended, until… death. And that is where our own death is something quite different from the death of others. If we are bereaved, we mourn a loss. With our own death, our life becomes complete, and to contemplate our own imminent death is to recognize that our life is becoming a whole, no longer possible to change. Heidegger argues that death is absolute in that it is the one thing that we have to experience for ourselves.

Insight

In other words, confronting death, you are absolutely and finally yourself. Nobody else can do it for you, nor can you pretend to be other than you are. It is as if all your possibilities have now collapsed into your own single reality.

People can all too often try to escape the reality of their lives by trying to conform to some external norm – to do 'what one ought to do'. Heidegger referred to this as *das Man-selbst* (the 'One-self'), and argues that this self always sees death as an *event*, as something that will happen one day in the future, but not something that affects my present life. He suggests that this is an evasion of the real issue here. We know that death is both inevitable, but also indeterminate; we know *that* it will happen, we just don't know *when*, and that influences how we see ourselves here and now.

Insight

Of all the possibilities I may see for my life, this is the one in which I am confronted with having to be absolutely myself, no longer able to escape into future dreams. The response to believing that you are soon to die is central to Sartre's wonderful short story 'The Wall' (see p. 151).

And, as we shall see in the next chapter, death holds a particular threat for Sartre, because it is the point at which we have to surrender ourselves to the judgement of other people, no longer able to change or influence what they think of us. At death, for the first time, we are fixed, our future having vanished.

Sartre also argued (in *Being and Nothingness*, p. 134, translation by Hazel Barnes, Routledge, 1958, 2003) that the past is the source of our present, and that when we die, we exist in the 'past' of those who survive us. Those who have no survivors, who are not remembered and therefore have no links with someone's present experience, are not 'past', they are simply annihilated. And that brings us to a key feature of existentialist thought, and of Heidegger's ontology, namely that our experience is always one of past, present and future; we live in time.

Being in time

An essential feature of Dasein is that it hopes and fears and plans. In other words, it lives forwards. To be defined entirely by your own past is, according to Heidegger, to think of yourself as a 'thing', a part of the world devoid of authentic human experience. The courage of his writing, and of the existentialism that was inspired by it, was to live forwards – aware of the past but not defined by it.

We shall examine the idea of 'authentic' and 'inauthentic' living in Chapter 5. For now, however, we should just be aware of the basis of living forwards. If you allow every decision to be determined by others, by circumstances, by your own history, then your life is 'inauthentic'. On the other hand, if you accept responsibility for choosing between the possibilities that life offers you, and take ownership of those choices, then you are living in an authentic way.

And this is where Heidegger's insight is so important for existentialism. We live within time, we have a past and a future – neither of which exist in the present moment except as a set of circumstances in which we find ourselves and a set of possibilities in terms of what we are to do. Our life is all about circumstances and possibilities – and that is what makes his ideas about living forwards so important. It is the challenge to own and choose, rather than to remain a victim of the past.

Insight

Time, for Heidegger, is not a sequence of 'nows', nor a measurement of change in a scientific sense. Rather, it is the personal framework of past and future within which we find ourselves living.

As always, it is Sartre who provides the best illustrations. In *Being and Nothingness* (p. 78) he describes a woman going out on a first date. She is determined not to be aware of the intentions of the man who is clearly chatting her up with some intention in mind. She concentrates only on the literal meaning of the compliments he pays her, ignoring the clear intention that lies behind the paying of such compliments. What the man says in this present moment is given meaning in terms of what he hopes will happen in the future! Meaning is time-related.

And this applies to many ordinary activities. Without a sense of time, we could never read a book. We would read only a single word. Reading a book implies the past (all the words that we have read so far) and the anticipation that we will continue reading. Sartre argued that a consciousness that was only conscious of what *is*, would have to spell out each word. There is nothing in the present moment that corresponds to reading the book.

Insight

The more we reflect on life, the more we see that the present only makes sense in terms of the past and future: all consciousness is related to time. The meaning of something cannot be the same as its scientific analysis in this present moment. We ask 'What's it for?' and immediately relate it to the future, and to the meaning and value that we give to things. This liquid only becomes a poison because of what it might do if I drink it!

In *Being and Time*, Heidegger sets out the groundwork for later existentialist philosophy. He sees people as engaged in a world that is shaped into 'my world' of meaning and significance, and which is lived forwards towards death. At every moment, our experience is that of personal meaning, of a past that is given and from which one is shaking free through present choices and concerns, and of a future which is partly given, and partly there to be shaped.

Heidegger suggests that there are three basic structures to Dasein: thrownness, concern and projection. They represent our circumstances, our engagement in the world, and the way in which we plan and hope for the future. This is not the sort of philosophy that Descartes or Hume would have recognized – for they were attempting to set out the logical and evidential basis for making statements about the world – nor is it a philosophy that sits easily with science, since science tends to see its own methodology as the sole means of achieving true statements about the world. But it is a philosophy that maps out the experience of being a human being. It looks at influences, concerns, anxieties, hopes, fears and so on. It is a philosophy that tends to address the most urgent of our questions about ourselves and the choices with which we are faced.

In this sense, existentialism is a philosophy for the streets, one that finds a natural resonance with ordinary people. And here we are back to the heyday of existentialist thought in 1945 Paris – a time of uncertainty but great hope, of people needing to think through what it means to be an engaged human being trying to make sense of one's own personal world.

10 THINGS TO REMEMBER

1 *Heidegger studies the human 'being there' ('Dasein').*

2 *Heidegger developed many of the key themes of later existentialism.*

3 *We are 'thrown' into a particular set of circumstances in this life.*

4 *Heidegger and existentialists reject the dualism of Descartes.*

5 *Existentialism builds on the phenomenology of Husserl.*

6 *Things may be seen as objects (present-at-hand) or tools (ready-to-hand).*

7 *We inevitably interpret the world from the perspective of our particular situation.*

8 *The scientific approach to understanding the world is secondary to that of the personal engagement.*

9 *At death our life is fixed and seen 'as a whole', rather than open to the future.*

10 *We live embedded in time, our meaning given by the past and the future.*

4

....

Existence precedes essence

In this chapter you will learn:
- *why 'nothingness' is so important for Sartre*
- *why we may suffer from existential 'angst'*
- *why Sartre saw hell as other people*

There is one idea that is absolutely central to existentialism: *existence precedes essence*. Understand that and everything else follows from it. But to grasp what a radical idea it is, we need to step back and look at the ideas of the ancient Greeks, particularly Aristotle.

For Aristotle, the *essence* of something is what makes it what it is. Know its essence and you know its place in the overall scheme of things, what it is for and what it should do. The essence of a knife is cutting, and a good knife is one that cuts well. To understand anything, it is necessary to explore its essence.

So, on the basis of that older philosophy, the key question was 'What is the nature (or essence) of humankind?' Once you know that, you know how humans relate to the rest of the world; you know how a person should understand his or her own life and its meaning and (if any) purpose. On that basis, you can also ask whether or not humans are free, and how they should act. For traditional philosophy, existence had always followed essence.

But the claim of existentialism is that, in the case of humankind, this is reversed. Your existence comes first and, by existing and acting, you determine your essence. You can no longer use your essence as your excuse; you take responsibility to shape your own life. That is the central idea and challenge of existentialism, and in this chapter we shall unpack some of its implications.

Although it received its definitive expression by Sartre, the implications of this key feature of existentialism are expressed succinctly by Merleau-Ponty in two sentences from the introduction to his *The Phenomenology of Perception*, published in 1945 (English translation by Colin Smith, 1962; see pp. xvi and xix):

▶ *'The world is not what I think, but what I live through.'*

and

▶ *'Philosophy is not the reflection of a pre-existing truth, but, like art, the act of bringing truth into being.'*

To create one's own truth in the world within which one lives, must have seemed attractively empowering, especially since the world was at that time torn apart by the Second World War and its aftermath, and millions of individuals found themselves tossed aside and left to perish. To ask 'What is my truth, and how may I live it?' must have seemed utterly new and empowering.

Like Kierkegaard arguing that truth is subjectivity, or Nietzsche insisting that humankind was no longer tethered to old systems of thought but was challenged to affirm its own future, so Sartre – with his phrase 'existence precedes essence' – expressed the key idea that it was *within the experience of living* that one's real self was to be discovered.

In 1947, Heidegger's *On Humanism* (responding to the publication the previous year of a book based on Sartre's famous lecture *Existentialism is a Humanism*) said that Sartre sums up Existentialism in the single principle 'existence precedes essence'. Heidegger pointed out that, in doing so, Sartre was rejecting the whole tradition of metaphysics. So let us focus again on this key phrase, and examine its significance.

Human nature is not fixed; there is no 'essence' of what it is to be a human being, to which we all ought to conform. 'Existence precedes essence' He implies that our nature is revealed in our existence – that it is our mode of being in the world that defines us, not some abstract or predetermined essence.

Heidegger's *Being and Time* was an analysis of Dasein's existence as engaged with the world. He saw the natural way to be in the world as 'being-with', relating to things – the very opposite of the Cartesian approach which was to stand back and attempt a detached analysis, as though that world were external to ourselves.

Insight

Heidegger claimed that, while rocks, horses or other things 'are', they do not 'exist' – in other words, that existence (as he describes it) is more than just being, it is living in the light of the 'nothing' that is our past and our future, or possibilities that shape our lives and give us our choices and our responsibilities.

What is clear is that I can choose between the possibilities that life throws up for me, but I do not have the freedom to choose absolutely anything, because those possibilities are always shaped by my circumstances. I am who I am because of what I have been, and because of the choices I have made in the past.

Here the contrast between the writing styles of Heidegger and Sartre could not be greater. Heidegger, exploring the nature of 'Being' uses his own definitions of words and strings them together to form a tapestry of ideas that only reveals itself with effort to appreciate each element woven into it. Sartre, by contrast, as a playwright is able to give concrete embodiment to the existential dilemmas. Issues of loyalty, defiance, and the unexpected turn of events all play their part in his dramatic works – but they are 'seen' rather than explained or examined.

Insight

To appreciate Sartre's existentialism, it is probably best to start by reading his novel *Nausea* (1938) or his short story '*The Wall*' (1939). These give a wonderful feeling for what existentialism is about. If your philosophy starts with people in actual situations, it is best shown by describing people in actual situations!

In this chapter we shall examine some key themes in *Being and Nothingness*, Sartre's major work, written under the influence of his reading of *Being and Time*. It is as near as one can get to the norm of existentialism, although there never was a single existentialist view but a constant debate within a circle of thinkers who had a common set of questions and a broadly similar approach.

Insight

Sartre's *Being and Nothingness* is almost as difficult and abstract as Heidegger in places, but Sartre's book is brought to life by his frequent illustrations of real life: the waiter who is trying to be a waiter; the voyeur who suddenly realizes that he is being spied on; the lady who tries to pretend to herself that the person across the table is not trying to seduce her. These, rather than the theorizing, bring existentialism to life.

Nothingness

One might imagine that this will be a short section, for what is there to say about nothingness? In fact, as used by Sartre, nothingness plays an absolutely central role in shaping who we are.

Every time I make a choice, I have to envisage that which does not exist. In other words, I have to imagine that I am now the possessor of what I contemplate buying, or married to the person to whom I am about to propose. What I am thinking about at that moment is not what already exists (for the present moment is an ever-diminishing fragment of time between past and future), but of what has been and is no more (the past) and what I might bring about by my choices (the future). But both of these have the character of nothingness – you cannot find the past or the future in terms of some kind of scientific analysis of who I am, since neither exist in the present moment; all you have are memory and anticipation.

Heidegger, whose examination of 'nothing' (*das Nichts*) sets the agenda for much of this thinking, made the idea of nothing central to his understanding of human reality. In the world of external objects, we have a place that is determined by our birth, location and death. But in the world as we experience it, the lived world of Dasein in which we participate, the key feature of our experience is nothing. After all, the past is nothing – but that is what makes us who we are. Equally the future is nothing – yet it is our projecting of ourselves into the future that constitutes our whole sense of hope, of action, or using things around us as tools to get a job done. The present moment only makes sense in terms of the nothingness of past and future. But neither past nor future is there in the present; the one has already ceased to be, the other is expressed in our intentions and hopes but is yet to be.

Looking for Pierre

In *Being and Nothingness* (p. 33) Sartre gives the example of going into a café where he has an appointment to meet Pierre. As he looks around for him, he negates all the things that appear before him, since they are not what he is looking for. He finally concludes 'Pierre is not here', but that does not mean that he has seen the absence of Pierre in some particular part of the café. The experience of the café becomes 'ground' upon which he seeks the 'figure' of Pierre.

This illustrates the way in which we are constantly searching for that which is not immediately presented to our senses. I go looking for precisely what I do not now see. I hope for what I do not now have. I desire what is not yet mine. Our engagement with the world is shaped by the nothingness which is past and future.

We can look at this in another way. At any one time human beings can turn their attention from what *is*, and consider what *might be*. We are concerned with that which does not at this moment exist – a nothingness that surrounds the existing present moment.

Insight

In everything we do, we look to a nothing. I am hungry – I intend something which does not at present exist: my eating a meal. I think of the next word to type on this keyboard; at the moment of thinking it, it does not yet exist. We are always aiming at that which we are not, at the 'nothing' which is future, while influenced by our own personal history, the 'nothing' which is past. If we were only aware of the present, life would be (literally) hopeless.

In fact, in a rigorous analysis the present becomes an infinitely small space as past moves into future. This is what Sartre calls the 'indissoluble dyad, Being and Nothingness' which gives him the title of his book.

Radical contingency

There is another aspect to nothingness – the realization that we just happen to exist, but could equally well not exist. We do not have to be here. This is illustrated by what is probably one of Sartre's best-known passages in his book *Nausea*. His principal character Roquentin suddenly sees just the solid existence of the things all around him – tree roots, hedges, gardens – and realizes that none of them is the reason for their own existence. But with that comes an equal awareness that I need not exist either.

Everything is absurd and superfluous. We are always aware of our own contingency. As Sartre put it (in *Being and Nothingness*, p. 104) 'we appear to ourselves as having the character of an unjustifiable fact.'

Angst

Kierkegaard described Angst as 'the dizziness of freedom', it is what happens when the familiar is removed and one is confronted with one's own freedom. It is a non-specific sense of anxiety, a feeling of being way out of one's depth and in deep, threatening water; it is the moment of leaving home, of facing the unknown.

Angst is not the same as fear. Fear is directed towards some object – if we are frightened, we are frightened of something, some person, object or event that we want to avoid. Angst is different, in that it is a general sense of being anxious, of feeling not-at-home in the world, of things generally not being right.

Angst is best illustrated by considering the way in which people escape from it. Heidegger (in *Being and Time*) suggests that they do so by hiding and trying to lose themselves in the world – what he calls 'falling'. It is a common phenomenon. People throw themselves into work, or a hobby, or a relationship, or some hopeless ambition. They seek to make success in that limited field a reason for living. Take away their work, or their family, or their status, and they feel utterly diminished, lost, uncertain about who they are anymore.

Angst is also experienced as we face the prospect of our own death – for that is the point at which one's being is exposed, no longer able to hide in some external source of comfort. Angst is what Heidegger called 'being-towards-death'. It is not dying that is the cause of Angst, but the fact that life is finite. We encounter Angst the moment we stand back and attempt to get an objective look at ourselves. We see our own finitude and the meaninglessness of the world around us.

Angst is the experience of the 'nothing', it is the sense that the world is slipping away from us. Angst also requires reflection. Fear can be an immediate, unreflecting response to an impending threat. But Angst is something more than that, it arises when we reflect on our situation (I may be ruined by this; I may be killed or wounded). To take Sartre's example (from *Being and Nothingness*, pp. 54–5), if I walk along a narrow path beside a precipice I fear falling off the edge, but may take steps to alleviate that fear by paying attention to where I put my feet. But I may also sense that these steps of mine may not be enough to prevent my falling. It is this that produces anguish (Angst) since I find myself in jeopardy.

Angst and world insecurity

Whether we think of Heidegger writing in the traumatic decade following the First World War, or Sartre during the Second, we should recognize that the background to existential thought (and to Heidegger's ontology that helped shape it) is a world that is all too aware of the utter fragility and uncertainty of life.

In many ways, the political and military traumas of the twentieth century naturally led people to ask fundamental questions about life and its meaning, but to be suspicious of any neat, ready-made answer. Faced with the real and imminent possibility of death, life takes on new and intense meaning. Angst is not simply fear of what is known, but that general sense that life is threatening and empty.

Within existential thought, Angst is related very closely to nothingness and to freedom. It is also the result of dispensing with a life dominated by 'doing the right thing' in terms of social expectations. Sartre referred to rules, signs, tax forms, policemen, as 'guard rails' against anguish. In other words, we use them to keep us from looking over and falling into an abyss of personal uncertainty. But for the person who contemplates his or her own freedom, all the guard rails collapse. In a conclusion that has implications for morality, Sartre says:

> *I emerge alone and in anguish confronting the unique and original project which constitutes my being... I have to realize the meaning of the world and of my essence; I make my decision concerning them – without justification and without excuse.*

And he concludes:

> *Anguish then is the reflective apprehension of freedom by itself.*
>
> Being and Nothingness, p. 63

Insight

Here we see the links in Sartre's thought. He starts by recognizing the *nothingness* that is a feature of my encounter with the world. That nothingness reveals my *freedom*, and

(Contd)

freedom produces *anguish (angst)* but also demands that we take *responsibility*. It seems to me that the real pivot point here is freedom; this is the central feature of existentialism.

The 'in-itself' and the 'for-itself'

Sartre's distinction between the 'in-itself' and the 'for-itself' is absolutely fundamental to his philosophy, because it represents two very different ways of existing in the world.

A non-conscious object exists 'in-itself': it is what it is and nothing more. The world of the 'in-itself' may be examined by science; it is the world of things.

To relate to the world as a human being, to be conscious and engaged, is to exist as 'for-itself'.

Insight

Sartre may have taken these terms from Hegel, who makes the distinction (in his *Lectures on the History of Philosophy*) between being 'in-itself' (*an sich*) as meaning one's potential, and being 'for-itself' (*für sich*) as meaning one's actuality. Both see the latter as coming with consciousness. It is curiously ironic to find this link between the builder of a great system of thought, and an existentialist who rebelled against all such systems.

A human being is always aware of a lack, of striving to be something more, of wanting to achieve a completeness that it does not yet possess. 'Human reality is, before all, its own nothingness' (*Being and Nothingness*, p. 112). If I consider only a thing (something in the world of the in-itself) then it is exactly what it is at this moment. It has a fixed self. But consciousness, the 'for-itself', is always aware of something more. To use Sartre's wonderful image, 'It is the full moon that confers on the crescent

moon its being as crescent; what-is-not determines what-is'
(*Being and Nothingness*, p. 111).

But – and this is the crucial difference between Sartre and religious
existentialists – he says 'But the being towards which human reality
surpasses itself is not a transcendent God; it is the heart of human
reality; it is only human reality itself as totality' (p. 114). So the
for-itself cannot be defined by its present, as can the things of the
in-itself, for it is always (to use two terms we shall examine later)
transcending its own **facticity**. It strives and understands itself
only in relationship to God (in religious existentialism), or human
reality as a totality (in the atheist form).

But – and this is the key to the whole existentialist approach to
authentic living, freedom and responsibility – there is always a
temptation for the 'for-itself' to want to define itself in terms of an
'in-itself.' To put it crudely: for consciousness to become a 'thing'.
In other words, there is a human craving to understand oneself as a
totality, as a defined and known entity. But this cannot happen, for
as soon as it tries to be fixed and defined, the 'for-itself' vanishes.
Hence, there is constant frustration, wanting to know ourselves
in a way that is impossible.

The temptation...

We so much want to 'be' someone that we are often tempted to
play at being someone. We take on a role – perhaps to do with
our work, or our place in the family, or our social position – in
the hope that it will give us meaning. In fact, putting on a mask
and acting the part is the one way to ensure that our real self
never gets a chance to develop. By doing so, we lose the very
thing we seek. We shall explore this further in considering what
existentialists mean by 'authenticity'.

We live forwards, we include in ourselves the 'nothing' that is all
we are not at the moment. Our past is the in-itself that we were at

that time but, of course, because we are still alive, that past in-itself is already being surpassed. It would be so tempting to see our whole life as a single 'thing' to which we could point and say 'Yes, that is absolutely me!' but it cannot happen. We are forced to be free, to choose what we will do, and to change ourselves in doing so.

Insight

The key thing to remember is that human beings always have a past and a future, they live in and through time. Isolated in the present moment, analysed, scanned, reduced to flesh and bones, neurons and hormones, even his or her DNA, a human being vanishes. It is never the object of scientific analysis. Human beings only appear in their existing, their continual process of moving forwards.

A bird in flight...

Sartre argues that, every time I am described in some way (as being a certain sort of person, or having some role), what is being described is already my *past*. If you want to shoot a bird in flight, you need to aim *ahead* of the bird rather than at it. So I cannot be described as I am in my present, for I am a constantly moving target. And it is my past that is my 'in-itself', or as Sartre put it (*Being and Nothingness*, p. 141) 'The past is the in-itself which I am, but I am this in-itself as *surpassed*.'

Some sentences in *Being and Nothingness* need to be read several times before they become clear! This is one of them: 'The for-itself is the being which is to itself its own lack of being. The being which the for-itself lacks is the in-itself. The for-itself arises as the nihilation for the in-itself and this nihilation is defined as the project towards the in-itself' (p. 586).

In other words, my consciousness is always looking towards the future, towards achieving something, making good some lack. I am not an object that can be defined, but at the same time I long to be defined (to be a certain, known, fixed thing). Human consciousness asks of life 'Is this it?' The existentialist answer appears to be both Yes and No; you can always transcend yourself, but you must also take full responsibility for everything you choose.

Insight

In other words, you are what you make of yourself, and the conscious you is the gap between the self that is now you and the self that you long to be.

Hell is other people

This, probably Sartre's best-known quote, comes at the end of his play *No Exit*, where the characters find themselves in hell, and realize that they need no further torture than what they are able to do to one another. But it reflects a key feature of part III of *Being and Nothingness*: the idea of 'being-for-others' – in other words, what I am as observed by other people.

We can treat people as objects, as performing a service for us, for example. But there are other occasions when we are aware that the other person is clearly in a position to take a view of us, and that we might become as much an object for them as they can be for us. Sartre illustrates this (p. 283) with an account of someone with his ear glued to a door, trying to overhear the conversation within, and then peeping through the keyhole. In the moment he does that, he is not conscious of himself, but totally engrossed in what is happening inside the room. Then, suddenly he becomes aware of someone behind him; he himself is being observed.

At that moment, Sartre observes, my sense of myself changes because I am also aware of being scrutinized and judged by another person.

I am no longer simply interested in what is happening beyond that door, I have become a 'peeping Tom.' Nothing else but another human being can give me that sense of personal embarrassment, shame or whatever.

That is a rather extreme example of a general situation, namely that we are always encountering and being encountered by other people. They take a view of us, see us as an 'object' within their world. Far from being a free 'for-itself' engaged in our world, we find that we are limited by the gaze of others; we suddenly become aware of ourselves in the mode of in-itself, as a thing. In the case of the 'peeping Tom', instead of simply observing, he now becomes exactly a 'peeping Tom', he is characterized. His self is narrowed into the in-itself world of objects (in this case, an object called a 'peeping Tom').

Of course, the self 'for-others' engages with other people in a number of different ways, sometimes dominating them, at other times being dominated, affirming ourselves but also watching and being aware of the way in which others perceive and define us.

As other people see me, I become an object for them. And I react emotionally to myself as seen by others – by feeling shame, for example – and accept their objective observation, their value judgements.

Insight

As we shall see, the crucial thing is whether this being for-others limits and distorts the self or enables it to develop in a positive way. Do other people constitute my hell, or the possibility of my heaven?

At death, the for-itself turns into an in-itself. In other words, it becomes something to be remembered, fixed and part of the past that people remember. It is no longer the forward living being that it was while alive. In *Being and Nothingness* (p. 138) Sartre says 'at the moment of death the chips are down, there remains not a card to play… At the moment of death we *are*; that is, we are defenceless before the judgements of others.'

What makes it so hard to think of oneself dead, according to Sartre, is that – until the point of your death – you can always assume that you can change, that whatever view other people have of you, it is always possible that they are wrong, and that you can be better than they thought, or different in some way. But from the perspective of death, change is no longer an option. You are, in the eyes of those who knew you, fixed for all time. There is nothing you can do now to change their opinion. That is why 'hell is other people' – not just that they are awful to live with, but that they are able to look at you and pass judgement. You are stuck with who you have been, rather than what you might hope to become.

Or, to put it in Sartre's philosophical terminology: 'By death, the for-itself has changed forever into an in-itself in that it has slipped entirely into the past' (*Being and Nothingness*, p. 138).

Insight

This idea is expressed wonderfully in Sartre's play *Les Jeux sont Faites* ('The Chips are Down'). The two principal characters in the play are killed off early on, and find themselves observing but unable to influence the on-going lives of others, causing them amazement and frustration.

But other people need not be hell, even for an existentialist. Gabriel Marcel, a Christian existentialist, brought in a new element, namely that the communication between people in a 'God-centred' community is the source of personal growth. In *Men Against Humanity* (1952) he argues that: 'It is only in groups that are restricted in number and animated by a spirit of love that the universal can be effectively embodied.' And he goes on to criticize the approach taken by Sartre for 'shutting ourselves within a nihilist consciousness of a sterile freedom.' This is the very opposite of Sartre's fear that hell is other people. Being with others is no longer a threat to the individual, but a positive enhancement.

Insight

For Sartre, love was really more a matter of wanting to be loved, or being seen as lovable by another human being. That is a

(Contd)

fundamental difference between his approach and the religious views of Marcel and Jaspers, for whom love is the key to, and perhaps the embodiment of, **transcendence**.

Marcel also criticized the mechanistic and impersonal nature of modern life, as missing out on the quest to understand the mystery of being. He feared the tendency of bureaucracy to reduce humans to a slip of paper to be sorted and filed, and was against any attempt to define people by statistics.

Although there is no scope to explore it here, one issue in assessing Sartre's view of relationships – and one that put him at odds with Marcel and Jaspers – is his view of love. In *Being and Nothingness* he explores the existential aspect of relationships in terms of masochism, sadism, hatred or indifference. Even in a passionate relationship motivated by desire, what you seek is not just the possession of another physical body, but of a free transcendent consciousness. Yet that is simply not possible. The other always eludes us, and always returns with a 'look' that makes us into an object. So, according to Sartre, there is something inherently frustrating in our relationships with other people.

Taking Paris by storm!

On 29 October 1945, Sartre gave a lecture entitled 'Existentialism is a Humanism'. Far from being a quiet and restrained affair, the crowds flocked in, clearly anticipating that this was going to be no ordinary philosophy lecture. Two years earlier, Sartre had published *Being and Nothingness*, which gave a systematic exposition of his existential philosophy, and he had already become known for his plays and novels, and for being an intellectual and writer who had supported the Resistance during the war. But it was this lecture that launched existentialism as a popular philosophy.

Sartre's aim was to defend existentialism against various complaints:

▶ *that it was a philosophy of quietism and despair, seeing action as ineffective;*

- ▶ *that it concentrated on the sordid side of human nature rather than the beautiful;*
- ▶ *that it considered individuals in isolation rather than in solidarity (a criticism made from a Communist point of view);*
- ▶ *that it dismissed eternal, God-given values and encouraged everyone to do what they liked.*

Aware that people regarded existentialism as something new and scandalous, he purported to explain that 'this is of all teachings the least scandalous and the most austere: it is intended strictly for technicians and philosophers.' But one wonders whether that was not simply a device for hyping up the anticipation of his audience, for he wanted to present his philosophy as one that was alarming because, above all, it 'confronts man with a possibility of choice' (page 2 of *Existentialism and Humanism*, the book that contains the lecture and some responses to it).

Sartre then outlined the basis of his theory that 'existence precedes essence' and boldly stated its implications for humankind: '... the first effect of existentialism is that it puts every man in possession of himself as he is, and places the entire responsibility for his existence squarely upon his own shoulders.'

As he unpacked various aspects of existentialism, he touched on many earlier philosophical and ethical theories. But all the time he kept coming back to the sense of personal responsibility – this was to be the key challenge, that there is no formula or principle by which one can measure one's life and assess it. What one *is* depends wholly on what one *does*.

And that – in a country with a history of Catholicism, and so recently torn apart by Nazi occupation, where the challenge of being a collaborator, a Resistance fighter, a communist, a Christian, an atheist, so readily provided people with convenient labels – offered a radical liberation from any battle of ideologies.

Sartre plucked arguments from Kant, ideas from Heidegger, referred to the subjectivity of Kierkegaard, and took the biblical figure of Abraham as one of his examples. He even identified his own starting point with Descartes' 'I think, therefore I am'. He added a lacing of well-crafted stories – like that of a young man, with a collaborator father and a needy mother, wanting to avenge the death of his brother in the German offensive of 1940, who is torn between leaving France in order to join the Free French Forces in England, and staying to look after his mother, whom he knows will be devastated by his leaving. In a complex set of values and loyalties, this story suggests, one simply has to *choose*; there is no easy way out or rule to follow.

Sartre returned time and again to this challenge – that we are forced to choose what we will do, and that 'you are nothing else but what you live' and that 'this theory alone is compatible with the dignity of man, it is the only one that does not make man into an object' (*Existentialism and Humanism*, p. 52).

And his language was clearly intended to engage his audience, rather than explore the subject in a detached, philosophical way: 'Life is nothing until it is lived; but it is yours to make sense of, and the value of it is nothing else but the sense that you choose.'

Insight

There is a nice play on the French here, for the sense you give to life is also the direction (in French *sens*) that you give it. Perhaps that typified the appeal of existentialism – that we make sense by giving direction, perhaps also thrusting (*asener*) forward, which comes from the same French root. Sartre took Paris by storm by offering a philosophy of direction and thrust.

Sartre also argued that existential humanism (unlike a humanism that takes man as an end in himself) implied that man was always, projecting himself forward, and that he (and she, although Sartre uses only the masculine form) lives by pursuing transcendent aims. In seeing man as 'self-surpassing' he was able to say that: 'There is no other universe except the human universe, the universe of human subjectivity' (p. 76). In other words, man *becomes* himself by always going *beyond* himself, creating his own values. It is in this sense that existentialism is a humanism, since it is focused on humankind as always free and open to the future.

And his final fling was to argue that, even if God were to exist (which, of course, he believed he did not) that would make no difference to the challenge to give one's life direction.

Insight

Existentialism and Humanism is often used as an introduction to Sartre's thought. It is short, clearly written, and a lot easier than *Being and Nothingness*. Yet Sartre was later to regret the content of that book and lecture. In many ways it shows Sartre plucking at issues, welding them together and constantly returning to his key theme. But it does not display the careful argument of *Being and Nothingness*, nor the immediacy of the issues that spring from his novels and plays. Still, for a first foray into existentialism, it gives a good 'feel' for what is it all about.

Heidegger was predictably critical. In *On Humanism*, he challenged Sartre's basic claim that 'existence precedes essence' gets beyond the world of metaphysics, by arguing that the reversal of a metaphysical sentence remains a metaphysical sentence. In other words, that although Sartre thinks he has now managed to get away from speculative knowledge, he nevertheless offers some kind of explanation of the world in doing so – he is still, in fact, doing metaphysics, trying to provide a rational explanation for things as they are.

Whatever the shortcomings of that particular lecture, it was *the* event for existentialism, the symbol that a new philosophy had arrived that would challenge people to take responsibility for their lives. People started calling themselves existentialists even if they knew relatively little about Sartre's philosophy.

So now, having explored something of the basic philosophy, we can turn in the next two chapters to how it was to be put into action – first in terms of living an authentic life, and then in terms of the challenge of freedom, choice and responsibility.

10 THINGS TO REMEMBER

1 'Existence precedes essence' is Sartre's key existential claim.

2 Our lives are shaped by 'nothingness'.

3 Angst is a response to freedom and to a sense of meaninglessness.

4 The world of things is 'in-itself'; consciousness is 'for-itself'.

5 We are 'for-others' when they see us as an object in their world.

6 We feel differently about ourselves when we know we are observed by others.

7 At death, we are fixed and vulnerable to the judgement of others.

8 Sartre's ideas may most easily be explored through his novels and plays.

9 'Existentialism is a Humanism' was the lecture that presented and defended existentialism as a popular movement.

10 Sartre emphasized freedom and responsibility as characterizing the implications of his philosophy.

5

The authentic life

In this chapter you will learn:

- *about what makes life authentic*
- *why we may be tempted to act in 'bad faith'*
- *why de Beauvoir wanted to free women from thinking of themselves as the 'second sex'*

> *Man is nothing else but what he makes of himself.*
>
> Sartre's 'Existentialism is a Humanism'

The reason for embracing existential questions was set out by Karl Jaspers in the opening of his *Philosophy*, published in 1932, in a chapter headed 'Philosophy starts with our situation', and it may serve to recap where we have come so far in our study of existentialism.

> *I do not begin at the beginning when I ask questions such as 'What is being?' or 'Why is anything at all? Why not nothing?' or 'Who am I?' or 'What do I really want?' These questions arise from a situation in which, coming from a past, I find myself.*
>
> (English translation E.B. Ashton, University of Chicago Press, 1969)

In other words, philosophy starts when I find myself in a world in which I need to take bearings. I look for answers that will give me support.

▶ *It is concerned with engaged human living, how we understand and respond to life, rather than a detached or scientific view of existence.*

▶ *It is concerned with consciousness, which is what distinguishes us from 'things'.*

▶ *Consciousness is always directed towards something – it is 'consciousness of'. It is not itself a 'thing'.*

▶ *Hence the danger of allowing ourselves to become 'things' rather than persons – to slip back into the world of the 'in-itself' rather than the 'for-itself'.*

▶ *To live the authentic life is to avoid this danger of becoming a 'thing'.*

These last two points lead us to ask what authentic living means and how it is possible.

In some sense, a concern with authentic living has always been a feature of philosophy since the time of Plato, but it was given particular emphasis by Kierkegaard who, in his book *Either/Or*, describes three stages of life:

1 *The aesthetic: superficially concerned with the senses.*
2 *The ethical: living in obedience to accepted moral standards.*
3 *The religious: moving beyond conventional morality into the realm of personal conviction, risk and anxiety.*

Moving into the third of these stages involves living without any external guarantees of security – it is striving to be yourself, without retreating into mere convention, or the superficial life of physical pleasure.

Heidegger speaks about authentic and inauthentic modes of living – a distinction taken up by Sartre in his discussion of what he calls 'bad faith', and exemplified by many of the feminist arguments put forward by Simone de Beauvoir.

The question of authenticity is central to the existential view of life. It is a matter of asking, with Karl Jaspers 'What does it mean to be human?' He argued that philosophy should be done while immersed in the historical process – as seeing, judging, choosing, reacting even. But in one of his later works (*Man in the Modern Age*) Jaspers argued against the idea that material progress in itself would provide happiness. Neither reason, nor science and technology can provide a recipe that satisfies a human being. Indeed, he tended to see true philosophy as emerging out of a failure of conventional reasoning. Just as Kierkegaard reacted against the vast rational scheme of Hegel in developing his philosophy of subjective risk, so Jaspers wanted to hold on to the importance of the subjective, and striving to explore a level of reality prior to the subjective/objective split.

Insight

Like many others, Jaspers refused to accept the label 'existentialist', and that is appropriate enough, because his philosophy is quite different from that of Sartre, with a clear emphasis on the ongoing human quest for transcendence, which he sees as a philosophical form of religion. Nevertheless, his interests are clearly existentialist in the broad sense of being concerned with the human *Existenz*.

So how is authentic life achieved?

Heidegger claimed, in *Being and Time*, that to exist authentically is to choose the possibilities of my existence. In other words, it is to be myself, and take responsibility for being myself, by selecting from the possibilities that life provides (in the situation into which I have been thrown). The opposite of this authentic existence is to do what 'one' does, to follow 'das Man' – in other words, to accept what is generally thought of as the correct thing, to accept the norms of society in an unquestioning way, falling back into what Kierkegaard called the 'ethical stage'. It is to refuse to take responsibility for your own free choices.

Affirming oneself

Nietzsche saw a dying of the old certainties, expressed in his language about the Death of God (in *The Joyful Science*, 1882). The world had become colder, less predictable, less comfortable. And in the face of that, his challenge was to create and affirm the Übermensch, the Superman, not as a fact, but as a choice. His works have been hugely influential, and not just for existentialists, in that they emphasize the challenge of human self-affirmation in a world where values and direction are not guaranteed, but have to be created – see particularly his *Thus Spoke Zarathustra* (1883–5) and *Beyond Good and Evil* (1886). We shall look at the ethical implications of this in the next chapter; for now let us just focus on the element of self-affirmation.

We need to get a feeling for that shift in awareness that Nietzsche heralded. Under a fixed order, in which the value of everything is related to a given and accepted structure, we know our place, and hence we know what we should do. When that old order fades, however, we are at a loss to value ourselves or anything, unless we do so on the basis of our will. We do not say, to use Nietzsche's image, that the Superman *is* the meaning of the Earth, but that the Superman *shall be* the meaning of the Earth. *In other words, value is given by the will, not discovered out there in the world.*

Insight

In considering the authentic life it is clear why existentialism is so indebted to Kierkegaard and Nietzsche, since the whole thrust of its challenge and popularity, in a world wrecked by world wars, was set by the twin themes of freedom and self-affirmation.

If we try to give ourselves meaning and direction in terms of the ordinary things with which we are surrounded, we end up 'falling' into the world of the 'in-itself' (to use Sartre's term) or the 'being at hand' (in Heidegger). In other words, we start to see ourselves, not as beings whose key character is freedom and consciousness, but as things, trapped in their place by other things.

There is a wonderful moment in Camus' story 'The Adulterous Woman' when, going out into the night while staying in a desert town in North Africa, the wife of a tired and failing businessman, looks up at the night sky. There – in an experience described in terms that resemble an orgasm – she finds herself totally at home beneath the stars in a vast and supremely beautiful universe. On returning to the hotel room and her sleeping husband, she lies down in the bed and weeps. There is a sense that her life has become so small, so confined to her very limited roles. Her adultery is not in a relationship with another man, it is in seeing herself as fully and authentically alive as a human being within a beautiful universe. The universe has brought her alive in a way her husband cannot.

All of that is a development of Nietzsche's saying 'yes' to life. And that has to be a 'yes' to a life that is finite – not one that somehow finds an external guarantee. For Nietzsche, the challenge of his 'eternal recurrence' is to say 'yes' to this life just as it is now, even if we knew that it would all be repeated over and over again for ever. Which brings us back to the fact that our life is finite and that we will have to face our own death. At death, we are confronted with being absolutely and finally ourselves.

Nazi self-affirmation?

Germany in the 1920s suffered the humiliation of the Versailles settlement following its defeat in the First World War, hyperinflation and a sense of complete national humiliation. The nation, like an individual, was therefore 'thrown' into a set of circumstances. How should it react? For Heidegger and others the question of how Germans might affirm their existence as a *Volk* must have seemed paramount.

(Contd)

For a short time (1933–4), Heidegger actively supported the Nazi Party. He argued that the university should not attempt disinterested learning, but should directly contribute to the natural development of the German people. He also saw the need for strong leadership to restore self-respect and self-affirmation to Germany. Unfortunately, that leadership was offered by Hitler and the Nazi Party – with results all too well-known.

Heidegger's titanic mistake does not detract from the value of his philosophy, but it cannot be ignored. It raises an important question about the nature of self-affirmation, whether it relates to an individual or to a nation: *To what extent is self-affirmation good in itself, irrespective of the goals that are chosen and affirmed? Are freedom, responsibility and commitment to be seen as good in themselves, or only in the context of the values to which the individual is committed?*

The essence of existential humanism, according to Sartre, is self-transcendence. In other words, at every moment, in every choice, a human being is able to become something more than what he or she was a moment before. We are constantly going beyond ourselves – a theme to which we shall return.

Concern

For Heidegger our engagement with the world is not all a matter of self-affirmation, and definitely not an attempt to put ourselves before other people. He makes this clear by his use of three words to describe our engagement – care (*Sorge*), concern (*Besorgen*) and concern for another (*Fürsorgen*). All three arise because, in his analysis of Dasein, Heidegger wants to make the point that we are naturally engaged and involved in the world, we do not simply stand back and observe it.

As so often, Heidegger uses terms in an unusual way. That is particularly true of 'care' (Sorge). We normally associate the word 'care' with emotional involvement and attachment, but for Heidegger it means something far more basic than that – the simple fact that we are 'thrown' into the world and engaged with it. Care is, if you like, the business of life that we attend to, that leads us to consider how to deal with problems and sort out the equipment that we have to hand for doing so. 'Care' is something more practical than emotional.

But he uses the term Fürsorgen to denote care that is shown towards another person. It describes the ability to think ahead for the welfare of that person, anticipating their needs, offering to relieve them and allow them to care for themselves. The aim of this, for the authentic life, is to allow the other person autonomy. By contrast a dominating concern for others, making them dependent upon us or subject to our particular will, he sees as a sign of the inauthentic life.

In the next chapter, looking at issues of freedom and responsibility, we shall see that Sartre and other existentialists also took the welfare of others into account. So whereas the idea of self-affirmation can (and sometimes does) suggest egocentric dominance, it does not necessarily do so – it can be an affirmation that says 'yes' to life as a whole, not just to one's own particular life.

Masks and bad faith

The enemy of authentic living is, according to Sartre, *mauvaise foie* (bad faith). This can simply mean self-deception, or lying to oneself. But it is rather more than that, because to lie implies that one knows the truth; to lie to yourself is, therefore, an expression of a cynical, rather than a mistaken consciousness. But how is this expressed?

Here Sartre comes to our aid with another of his illuminating examples (in *Being and Nothingness*, p. 82). He observes a waiter in a café and sees that his actions are all a little too contrived, precise and rapid. He is actually a waiter in a café, but at the same time he is playing at being a waiter in a café. He is trying to follow a role, to act out his part perfectly, and therefore it all looks a bit strained. He is not being authentic, not being himself.

Similarly he argues that people expect a grocer, tailor or auctioneer to be nothing but that. They are expected simply to act out the role for us – we see them as 'things' in our world. Even more so the soldier, who is required to act the role without any thought of self, even to the point of putting his or her life at risk. Bad faith is accepting and pretending that one is nothing but that role, allowing oneself to be no more than a 'thing', part of the 'in-itself' world.

Insight

Of course, other people may need to see me in role. I'm no use as a waiter unless I actually do my job. The situation becomes bad faith, and I slip into an inauthentic mode of being, when I myself accept myself as only acting within that role. In other words, it is the point at which I identify entirely with the social mask I wear.

Bad faith involved deliberately denying something we know to be true of ourselves; it is an attempt to escape from our own anxiety about the ambiguity of our lives. In other words, it is the point at which a person chooses to identify himself or herself entirely with his or her 'being-for-others'.

Notice what Sartre is doing here. He is using a practical example in order to make his point. You 'see' what the waiter is doing, and are therefore aware of the gap between the waiter and his reality. That is down to the method of phenomenology – exploring what is seen in our experience, rather than setting up a theoretical framework. Sartre has a wonderful way of using his literary talent to enable us to see what he sees and thereby understand what he means.

Insight

Insight

It is a sad fact that, once you 'see' the waiter, you start to see examples of bad faith all around you. In the 1970s there was a television series called *The Fall and Rise of Reginald Perrin* in which Leonard Rossiter brilliantly portrayed a suburban middle-class manager, utterly bored with his work and social role, who finally freaks out, fakes his own death and disappears into a new life of freedom. Recently re-made, and starring Martin Clunes in the title role, it portrays the escape from bad faith into authenticity – except not exactly, for Reginald Perrin only ever conformed with tongue in cheek, never having been wholeheartedly a cog in his company or domestic wheel.

Similarly, in *Being and Time*, Heidegger sees the danger of doing as 'one' (*das Man*) does – in other words, following what is socially expected, rather than choosing for yourself how you will live – as an escape mechanism, avoiding the responsibility of choice. He also speaks of the 'fallenness', a state of being lost in the world of things and tasks and occupations, living exclusively by adopting the ready-made roles one is offered.

Of course, many will stay in this 'fallen' state rather than face the Angst of accepting freedom, responsibility and the challenge and uncertainty of an authentic life.

Key to escaping bad faith is the recognition that we are actually free. Only if we deny freedom do we slip back into a world of 'things' and bad faith, where everything we do appears to be the product of external causes and constraints.

Insight

To complain 'But I have no choice!' is to be 'fallen' and in bad faith. As we shall see in the next chapter, Sartre argues that we are condemned to be free, whether we wish to be or not; we always have a choice.

Freud and the Rear-view Mirror

Sigmund Freud (1856–1939) is revered as the inventor of psychoanalysis and, if more disputably, the discoverer of the Unconscious. Although Freud considered himself primarily a scientific physician, not a philosopher or writer, his medical reputation has not survived as well as his mythopoeic writings. Phrases like 'Oedipus complex', 'the Unconscious', 'repression' and 'Freudian slip' have entered our vocabulary, but Freudianism as a practical discipline seems to be in retreat.

In the 1920s Freudian ideas were taken up enthusiastically by surrealist artists. Led by André Breton, they claimed to paint only what their unconscious suggested. Freud dismissed such claims, saying witheringly that while with most painters he sought the unconscious motive behind the conscious art, with the surrealists he looked for the conscious intent behind the supposedly unconscious work. Later, philosophers such as Herbert Marcuse (1898–1979) fused Marxism and Freudianism in a revolutionary mixture that had heady erotic appeal in the 1960s.

Freud had no appeal to the existentialists, however. This was not because of his insistence on the importance of sex but because existentialists reject the Freudian division of the mind into separate conscious/subconscious levels, with the Id cast as the repressed primal self, lurking in the Unconscious like a child-molester in a cellar. For existentialists, what is not conscious does not really exist. Consciousness for them is 'translucent', open to its own viewing. Freud's negative view of the Id reflected his own pessimism about the human condition. He saw our choices as dictated by neuroses that, due to their formation in infancy, we can never extirpate. Instead, we must live peeping back horrified at our earliest experiences, as if in the mind's rear-view mirror. Existentialists, by contrast, preach human freedom and look forward, not back.

So, for an existentialist, there is no escaping responsibility by arguing that everything is determined by the promptings of the unconscious. When it comes to 'inauthenticity', 'bad faith', and 'fallenness' we have no excuse.

The roles of women

One is not born a woman, but becomes one.

Simone de Beauvoir, *The Second Sex*

Simone de Beauvoir's *The Second Sex*, published in 1949, has been a hugely influential and very popular book, articulating the injustice of women's place in a world dominated by men and encouraging liberation and authenticity.

She explores the way women have been seen historically, and questions why they have accepted the role of being the 'second' sex, defined in terms of their relationship to men – as wife, mother, daughter, lover. There is a sense, seen perhaps in the assumptions of many characters in Jane Austen's novels, that a woman becomes somebody only when a man takes notice of her, and provides her with a role and a place in society. Long before de Beauvoir, Austen, George Eliot and others, were exposing this relative nature of women, and starting to affirm their heroines as women in their own right, independent of the social world created by men.

In *The Second Sex* she offers a *social* critique of the position in which women find themselves. They are prevented from adopting existentialist freedom because they are expected to conform to social views about what is expected of women. In other words, the temptation for an individual to live in bad faith, or to adopt a mask, is a *social phenomenon not simply an individual one*. Therefore, in order to effect change – even if that change happens one person at a time – there needs to be a change in the way that society as a whole views the place of women.

Gender is generated by the accepted conventions of society; it is part of the given in the world into which every female is 'thrown' at birth. And like all such conventions, it can be challenged and changed.

Key to her thinking is the central existential doctrine that existence precedes essence – in other words, a woman is what she makes of herself, she does not have some eternal, fixed essence to which she must conform. This is crucial, for if there is a distinctive feminine essence, women can be expected to adopt roles that reflect that essence. On the other hand, if existence comes first, then women are free to develop their own nature by the free choices that they make, unfettered by prior ideas of essence. This feature of existentialism applies equally to men and to women, but the interesting thing about de Beauvoir's work is that it highlights the fact that women seem to require their place to be examined, whereas men would take their place for granted.

Insight

If that is no longer the case today, it is down in no small part to the influence of *The Second Sex* and the feminist movement. Back in 1949 women were far more likely to feel themselves in a subservient role vis-à-vis men, although the war must already have shifted that perception significantly, since women had found themselves doing work previously considered part of the male domain.

Of course, not all women have wanted to be liberated. Why might that be so? It seems that there is a constant temptation to settle for the mask, the role, and particularly the easy option of seeing oneself as a 'thing' rather than as a free consciousness. That may be true of individual men and women, but de Beauvoir adds (in a way that Sartre does not) a social dimension to this. Society itself tends to operate in terms of groups, and thus individuals come under pressure to conform. Liberation is therefore needed for a whole class of people, rather than simply for individuals. Although Sartre was happy to say that one was 'condemned to be free' whatever one's situation, de Beauvoir observes that some women are so oppressed in their subservient role that they cannot imagine themselves otherwise. For them, society needs to change before they can take charge of their own free choices and have a new view of their future. Apart from anything else, she observed that women were unable to identify themselves with their own sex, so they do not find themselves in a position to affirm themselves against men (as, for example, one social class might be aware of its oppression of another in a Marxist social analysis).

Insight

De Beauvoir's work highlights the balance between the individual and society and raises questions for existentialism: How do you change individuals without also changing the society within which they live? Are you personally responsible for living in bad faith, or wearing a mask, if that is the expectation of the society into which you are born?

If existentialism is about the courage to live an authentic life, shaking off traditional masks and affirming oneself in one's free choices, then it developed at exactly the right moment for women, and its impact on the social relations between the sexes has been deep-rooted and lasting.

Courage and reason

Heidegger, Sartre and de Beauvoir all see adopting an established role, or mask, as the easy way out. To be authentic, to be in the 'for-itself' mode, or to be a woman, requires courage and an attitude which accepts one's own situation and is willing to take responsibility for it.

Courage is often associated with facing the prospect of death. Heidegger makes the point that the inauthentic self (the *Man-selbst*) sees death as an event that will happen at some point in the future, but which does not trouble the present; in other words, it tries to avoid death as a possibility for my being here and now. One dies, but not yet. But from an existentialist perspective, death is the one certainty that is also indeterminate; we know *that* it will happen, but not *when*. Courage is facing that certainty and allowing it to give us a new perspective on our life, for it allows us to see ourselves as 'that is what I was'. To accept that (as we saw in terms of 'hell is other people') is never easy, for it is the only occasion when we are utterly exposed as we are, without the prospect of putting the record straight or claiming that we have a potential that is as yet undiscovered.

Taking death into account?

Sartre emphasizes the fact that death may suddenly and randomly cut us off, and therefore that death cannot be part of our view of life, since, as Epicurus said, death is not something we experience, and therefore not something that we need to take into account.

But is it possible to live without taking one's own death into account? If those condemned to die in the morning see their life differently in the light of their coming execution, is it not equally reasonable for people to live in permanent awareness that one day they will die?

We have already considered Nietzsche's affirmation of life, saying 'yes' to it just as it is. That too requires courage. Life requires courage, especially of those who do not fit in with their expected roles, who live and act in their own way, rather than following what might be expected of them. That was certainly the case with Nietzsche himself, for he did not conform to the norms of philosophy or academic life.

Nietzsche: the philosopher as prophet and poet

'Of all writings I love only that which is written with blood. Write with blood and you will discover that blood is spirit,' wrote Nietzsche (*Thus Spoke Zarathustra*). These are strange words for a philosopher, usually thought a cerebral profession. But, while now recognized as one of the greatest of all thinkers, Nietzsche hardly *was* a philosopher in the normal sense. He did not study philosophy at university and the chair he accepted at Basel University in 1869, aged only 24, was in classical *philology*, Greek and Latin. Later he applied for the philosophy chair at Basel – in vain. Soon he became too ill to teach anyway. Pensioned off at just 34, he spent his last (sane) decade wandering alone in the Alps and Mediterranean, writing madly but hardly being read at all.

Most of his works were written in an aphoristic polemical style with a very unacademic excitement. Instead of setting out hypotheses to be debated in an air of supposed detachment, Nietzsche used a range of rhetorical effects to dazzle or arouse readers, like an actor or poet. (He also wrote fine lyric poetry, still read today.) *Thus Spoke Zarathustra* is almost operatic in its hyperbole and rich imagery: 'It is night: now do all leaping fountains speak aloud. And my soul too is a leaping fountain… All joy wants the eternity of all things, wants honey, wants dregs, wants intoxicated midnights'. No other philosopher ever wrote like this. For his later books, he switched to an increasingly pithy style. 'How to say in a book what others say in ten books – what others do *not* say in ten books,' was his ambition.

In this he was emulating the Pre-Socratics (Greek philosophers before Socrates) notably Heraclitus (*c.*500 BCE). Heraclitus was famed for enigmatic, sibylline aphorisms: 'All is change, nothing is motionless'; 'Character is destiny'; 'The path up is the same as the path down'.

(Contd)

Nietzsche also often wrote in ambiguous aphorisms. He made no attempt at systematic philosophy – he thought the desire for a system such as Hegel's and Kant's showed a 'lack of [moral] integrity.' He was also a penetrating psychologist – Freud acknowledged him as such – an iconoclast and prophet. 'If one had the smallest degree of superstition left, one would be unable to ignore the idea that one is merely incarnation, mouthpiece, medium of overwhelming forces,' he declared in *Ecce Homo*, the autobiographical work written in late 1888, the last weeks of his sane life. The words make a suitable epitaph for a man who was never merely an academic philosopher.

Courage is also required to step outside the comfort zone of reason. Authenticity requires that we deal with the immediate situation, not some absolute ideal. It is made more difficult because the world never fits in with our expectations, not what we think it should be. The problem is that we want to live reasonably in a world that is reasonable, but reality refuses to comply with our expectations. The existentialist rejects the rationalist presupposition, recognizing that we have to deal with the world just as it is, and take responsibility for the choices we make in it. We cannot excuse ourselves on the grounds that the world has not provided what we would have liked.

The absurd thing is that the world is not reasonable; indeed, we would have no reason to call the world absurd if we did not assume that a reasonable world would be at least possible. There is therefore a gap between the human longing to make sense of the world, and our experience of it.

Insight

Philosophers have always been divided on the matter of the reasonableness of things. Among the Greeks, the Stoics were of the view that the whole universe was ruled by a single principle of reason – the 'logos' – whereas the Epicureans thought that everything was a matter of chance and the interlocking of a series of impersonal laws of nature. Indeed, philosophers have continued what we may call the 'chance vs necessity' debate ever since.

The modern dilemma is that science shows us a world that is both reasonable (in the sense that it is predictable rather than capricious) and impersonal. That may be intellectually satisfying from the standpoint of an objective view of things – a study of the 'in-itself' – but it does not really help to address the existential questions, as the 'for-itself' courageously seeks to create meaning and value.

A scientific view of life?

It is still often assumed that the task of philosophy is to understand eternal verities, whereas that of science is to understand the world in a cool, objective, disinterested way. Indeed, scientific method aims to eliminate all subjectivity from the analysis of experimental results. Of course, we now know that all scientific theories involve a measure of personal interpretation, and that theories compete against one another, sometimes offering equally valid ways of seeing the phenomenon under examination. But that does not detract from the almost universal assumption that to be 'scientific' is to try to get to the truth, unhindered by personal preferences and interests.

Hence the radical departure when Kierkegaard proclaimed that subjectivity is truth, and explored issues of responsibility, choice, commitment, inwardness and so on. He was deliberately unscientific – and saw that as essential if the personal questions about human life were to be tackled in an adequate way.

Hence the existential quest for authenticity is quite different from a scientific exploration of human life. Whereas psychology, sociology, neuroscience and so on attempt to give an objective view of life, existentialism always preserves the experience of authenticity against any attempt at scientific reduction.

So courage is required to address a world that does not conform to one's reasonable expectations. There are some periods of history where courage, or the lack of it, is more clearly visible than others. Some (perhaps all) of the thinkers we have been examining battled with internal and personal dilemmas, but they also have in common the background of a world in a state of change or trauma.

Nietzsche's work probes the implications in changes of belief and attitude in nineteenth-century Europe. Heidegger's work has as its backdrop the trauma of the First World War, and the terrible state of the German economy in the 1920s. If he wanted to give individuals, the university and the German *Volk* a sense of courage and self respect, it was because he felt they were lacking, in a situation where it would be all too easy to be swamped by despair and nihilism.

Sartre studied Heidegger's *Being and Time*, and drafted his own *Being and Nothingness* while incarcerated in Stalag 12D prisoner-of-war camp, the quintessential setting for asking existential questions. A forged certificate, claiming disorientation due to partial blindness in his right eye, gained him his freedom to return to Paris where he wrote *Les Mouches* (*The Flies*), a pro-Resistance play, as well as finishing his *Being and Nothingness* and the first two volumes of his *Roads to Freedom* trilogy. This is no ivory tower philosophy, but one forged in a world under Nazi occupation, where courage was constantly in demand.

The existentialists were not provided with a comfortable, reasonable world.

10 THINGS TO REMEMBER

1 *Existentialism starts from our situation in the world.*

2 *It goes beyond conformity to ethical or social rules.*

3 *It requires self-affirmation, and saying 'yes' to life.*

4 *Affirmation is not necessarily self-centred, it may involve concern for the welfare of others.*

5 *We may be tempted to escape authenticity by adopting a role or mask.*

6 *Simone de Beauvoir highlighted the social aspect of women's struggle for authenticity.*

7 *It requires courage to refuse to conform to the expectations of others.*

8 *The world may seem absurd only if it might also have been seen as reasonable.*

9 *The existentialists wrote against a background of social and political trauma.*

10 *Authenticity is the refusal to become a 'thing' and to sink into bad faith.*

6

Freedom, choice and responsibility

In this chapter you will learn:
- *to consider whether freedom is real or illusory*
- *why we construct our own morality*
- *why all ethics involves a fundamental ambiguity*

> *Life is nothing until it is lived; but it is yours to make sense of,
> and the value of it is nothing else but the sense that you choose.*
>
> Sartre *Existentialism and Humanism* (translated by Philip Mairet)

What do you do when all the old certainties are removed, when the world presents itself as fragile, full of hazards, offering you an uncertain future or perhaps no future at all? What can you hold onto and commit to in a world where global financial crises may drain your savings or your future pension, where redundancy may threaten your lifestyle or take your home from you, when loved ones die, or friendships turn sour?

One option is to become a nihilist, to say that nothing has (or can have) value. Another is to take the less pessimistic but more challenging route of admitting that meaning and value are created rather than discovered, and to acknowledge that the choosing and committing is what gives life meaning. This was the option taken by Nietzsche and the majority of existentialist thinkers.

So the existentialist challenge was to reject external authority and all forms of social convention and to live purposefully in the light of your own values and self-understanding. That offers freedom, but also brings responsibility; taken seriously, it was never going to be an easy option.

In this chapter, we shall be looking at what existentialist authenticity involves in terms of freedom, responsibility and ethics. I cannot choose the circumstances of my life, but I can choose how I will react to them. For Sartre, that gives me a measure of freedom and responsibility and sets the challenge of existentialism.

Insight

We need to keep a balance here between the tendency of some existentialists to see the world as utterly devoid of value and meaning and therefore as absurd (a nihilism of which Camus, for example, has been accused) and an over-optimistic view of the ability of people to affirm and shape their own future (an extension of Nietzsche's 'yes' to life).

Freedom: illusion or reality?

The problem of freedom is one that has long concerned philosophy. One may believe oneself to be free to choose, but from the standpoint of the external observer, that freedom is an illusion. The task of science is to find reasons for everything that happens. These may be physical, social or psychological. My therapist will assure me that my decision was quite predictable; an economist will see my decision to withdraw money from my bank as merely one example of an inevitable trend within the economy.

It is even theoretically possible that, at some point in the future, perhaps as a result of advances in neuroscience, we will be able to explain every choice in terms of antecedent neural activity. At that point, it might seem nonsense to speak of human freedom, or to ascribe praise or blame to any actions. But we do not need to wait for a perfect neuroscience to explain all aspects of human behaviour, we already relate criminality to social deprivation and violent behaviour to early upbringing. In court there are always mitigating circumstances. That might suggest that freedom is an illusion.

But all such views treat the self as an 'in-itself' (to use Sartre's term). In other words, they treat it as an object within the world of phenomena. But the freedom that is celebrated by existentialists is the freedom of the 'for-itself', the experience of freedom in choosing and acting to shape its own future. 'Man does not exist *first* in order to be free *subsequently*; there is no difference between the being of man and his being-free' (Sartre, *Being and Nothingness*, p. 49).

Kierkegaard described a kind of dizziness that came with the experience of free choice, a choice made in the context of (as the title of one of his books has it) 'Fear and Trembling'. Whatever philosophy and science may have to say about human freedom, it is certainly *experienced* as real, and that is what counts for existentialism.

But our relationship with freedom is ambivalent. Sartre saw man as 'a useless passion' because he was always wanting to be free, while at the same time wanting to find in himself some fixed essence and to identify himself with the objective 'in-itself' world.

Insight

In a sense, when it comes to freedom, you can't have it both ways – either you grasp freedom and take the risk of absurdity and lack of meaning, or you avoid the responsibility of being free, accept social, psychological and scientific determinism, and see your authenticity vanish into conformity.

For Sartre, we are 'condemned to be free'; it is not an option. We can only attempt to escape it by retreating back into the world of things (the in-itself), denying the key feature of human consciousness. Whatever my circumstances, I can always opt out of them.

But Maurice Merleau-Ponty takes a rather different slant on freedom, pointing out that it is related to things we are committed to doing. Thus, for example, if I decide to walk up a flight of steps, it will never be achieved if, at each step, I claim the freedom to change my mind and walk down again!

Insight

If we are free all the time, what would it mean not to be free? If we are always free, even in the most restricting of circumstances, what is it that impels us to take the step of claiming our freedom, rebelling against our situation or defying convention? To say to a prisoner that he is really free because he could opt out through suicide, does not seem to me to describe what most people mean by freedom.

Freedom is always experienced in a context. Most of the time I simply continue with what I am doing, following well-established habits. I continue walking, putting one foot in front of the other; I drive my car down one road after another. It is not that I am forced to do so, but what I do follows my previous decisions and projects. Indeed, for most of us most of the time, that is how we get through our days; we do not stop and ask if we are free or constrained, for we know that, in our circumstances, we have a measure of freedom within limits that we ourselves have sometimes chosen, or perhaps circumstances or other people have chosen for us.

The philosopher Isaiah Berlin made the important distinction between 'freedom from' and 'freedom to'. We may wish to be *free from* restraints and limitations, but also *free to* explore and bring about our own chosen ends. Merleau-Ponty's point appears to be that we may well wish to be *free from* before we are able to be *free to*, in that people are repressed before they revolt and claim the freedom to seek their own ends. So whereas for Sartre freedom is absolute, and belongs to a quite different realm from physical restraint, Merleau-Ponty sees freedom and restraint as a matter of degree and a mixture.

Facticity and transcendence

These two terms set the context for the existentialist view of freedom and morality:

▶ *Facticity – the given circumstances of our life. We cannot escape our facticity; we are always embedded in life.*
▶ *Transcendence – our ability to look beyond our situation, to make choices, to set goals, to use our will to shape our world.*

Both of these are essential for existentialism, simply because it is a philosophy based on engagement with the world. If we see only our facticity and try to deny our transcendence, we fall into what Sartre called 'bad faith'. Without transcendence, we pretend that we are no more than a 'thing' among other things, causally determined. But if we attend only to our transcendence and attempt to deny our facticity, we fall into a Cartesian dualism that separates off the self from the world, and that can lead us to speculate about a 'real' self that is quite other than our actual circumstances.

At a basic, existential level, we can ask ourselves two questions:

1 *Am I what life has made me?*
2 *Am I what I want to become?*

The first is about my facticity, the second about my transcendence. To live an authentic life, it is important that I accept *both*. It is that tension between the given and the wished-for that sets out the possibilities of our life.

In part IV of *Being and Nothingness*, Sartre gives useful summaries of his argument. He emphasizes that every act projects the self towards nothingness, towards what is not; in other words, the self sets itself goals, chooses what it wants to happen. Things may get in my way, but they cannot determine who I am or what I choose for myself. Freedom is not simply an *aspect* of being me, it is *what it means* to be me. I cannot be sometimes a slave and sometimes free – I am always free, whether I like to acknowledge it or not.

Insight

I may think that, simply because someone is holding a gun to my head or I am in prison, I lose my freedom. Not so, according to Sartre. However limiting my situation may be, I am free to decide how to respond to it.

Now, one may well argue that I am not totally free; life does indeed provide me with limitations, I cannot do anything I want. Notice however that the freedom that Sartre insists on in *Being and Nothingness* is not the freedom to *achieve* what we want, but to *choose* what we want. Sartre holds that even our emotions and passions are free, because they are intentional – in other words, they relate to what we wish for in dealing with the person or object before us.

Insight

My personal view is that Sartre overstates this position. We often respond to what is presented to us. Our senses are stimulated and emotions are engaged. We may be free in terms of our expression of those emotions, but we are hardly in control of the mechanism by which they come about in the first place. In the case of a compulsion, we may feel dominated by emotional longings that are beyond our conscious control.

Nevertheless, in terms of human consciousness, we are not objects determined by scientific laws. According to Sartre we are *condemned* to be free and *abandoned* in the world.

Responsibility

Responsibility is something you cannot escape. Kierkegaard made the important point that you have to take responsibility for making a choice, and that you are equally responsible if you refuse to make a choice, because you allow what happens to be determined by circumstances rather than by your act of will. Letting nature take its course is still a choice for which you are responsible.

According to Heidegger, it is always tempting to avoid responsibility by following 'das Man' (Man), in other words, by doing what is expected of you. But that is seen by existentialists as a cop out – we are free and responsible, and it is no good following orders or blaming circumstances.

This was expressed succinctly by Beckett in *Waiting for Godot*, where Vladimir says to Estragon: 'There's a man all over for you, blaming on his boots the faults of his feet.'

Therefore, whether we refer to it as adopting a mask, or living in bad faith, or inauthenticity, it amounts to the same thing – refusing to take personal responsibility and blaming our situation on the various 'boots' that we have, whether they be our background, economic circumstances, genetic predisposition, the limitations of the political situation, friends, family or whatever. They are all 'boots', whereas the existentialist will consider nothing but the responsibility of the feet within them.

If you think of yourself as nothing more than an object, science – in the form of psychology, sociology, economics or neuroscience – may offer you a perfect set of excuses for what you do. But for existentialists that would be to fall into 'bad faith.' And here we return again to that pair of concepts used by Sartre: facticity and transcendence. To deny either of these is to fall into bad faith. To hold them together is to take responsibility – neither stuck with the 'facticity' of what life has given us, nor totally given over to dreaming of 'transcendence', but recognizing that we have responsibility for taking the step of choosing what to do, of deciding how we will relate to the world.

Insight

Perhaps the simplest way of looking at this is to say that existentialism challenges us to balance our dreams against our facts, neither using our circumstances as an excuse, nor detaching our dreams from reality.

In part IV of *Being and Nothingness* Sartre has a section entitled 'Freedom and Responsibility'. In it he makes some remarkable claims:

▶ that man, '*condemned to be free carries the whole weight of the world on his shoulders*';
▶ that we are responsible for everything that happens;
▶ that whatever happens has meaning for us in terms of our own personal 'project'.

Let us take his most dramatic example (particularly poignant for anyone writing in 1943):

> **If I am mobilized in a war, this war is my war; it is in my image and I deserve it. I deserve it first because I could always get out of it by suicide or by desertion; these ultimate possibles are those which must always be present for us when there is a question of envisaging a situation. For lack of getting out of it, I have chosen it.**
>
> *Being and Nothingness* (pp. 574–5)

He even agrees with the view that in war there are no innocent victims. 'If therefore I have preferred war to death or to dishonour, everything takes place as if I bore entire responsibility for this war ... For it depended on me that for me and by me this war should not exist, and I have decided that it does exist.'

Insight
It is true that we give value and meaning to all we encounter, and that we could opt out of everything through suicide. But that does not mean that we determine *what* we experience, merely *that* we experience it. Perhaps, to be fair to Sartre, what his argument implies is simply that we are responsible for what we make of every situation, even if that situation is a war. I do not create the war, but I do decide what I shall make of it.

Sartre ends this section of *Being and Nothingness* by saying that everything in this world is an opportunity or a chance. In this,

his language veers towards that of a modern self-help book: every problem is an opportunity; every disaster, a chance to learn and to grow. However terrible life may seem, we have a responsibility to ourselves to make something of it.

At the end of his *The Phenomenology of Perception*, Merleau-Ponty highlights the existentialist claim that one must take responsibility by saying that it is: '... by plunging into the present and the world, by taking on deliberately what I am fortuitously, by willing what I will and doing what I do, that I can go further'.

And that encapsulates the essence of what the existential life is about; it is the position of affirmation from which I can move forward.

Constructing morality

In *Existentialism and Humanism*, Sartre sees moral choice as being like the construction of a work of art: it is the creative process of shaping our lives and thereby showing our values. You are free to choose what to do, and required to take responsibility for that choice. Morality, then, is something to be constructed.

But he also seems to come improbably near to promoting the ethics of Immanuel Kant, that great philosopher of the European Enlightenment and advocate of a supremely rational approach to life. Sartre argues that, in choosing for yourself you are in effect choosing for everyone else as well.

His argument here is very clear; it can be summed up in this way:

- ▶ *If you act to create yourself, you also create an image of what you believe a man (or woman) should be;*
- ▶ *To make a choice is to affirm the value of what is chosen;*
- ▶ *We always choose what we see as better for us, and therefore, by implication, for everyone;*

- *As we choose, we shape an image that is valid for everyone;*
- *Hence our responsibility is great, because it concerns a choice for 'mankind as a whole'.*

He concludes by claiming that: 'In fashioning myself I fashion man' (*Existentialism and Humanism*, p. 33).

He is therefore prepared to ask of an action 'What would happen if everyone did so?', which sounds like a rather basic version of Kant's first form of the Categorical Imperative (namely that you should be prepared to will that the principle upon which you act should become a universal law), and he even argues that:

When a man commits himself to anything, fully realizing that he is not only choosing what he will be, but is thereby at the same time a legislator deciding for the whole of mankind – in such a moment a man cannot escape from the sense of complete and profound responsibility.

And this almost exactly reflects Kant's third form of the Categorical Imperative.

Insight

It seems to me that Sartre wants to suggest that the challenge of existentialism is, in some way, heir to the whole European tradition that stems from Kant. The implication of taking existential commitments seriously is that one follows the rational principles of Kant. Whether Kant would have agreed with Sartre is quite another matter!

What cannot be in doubt, however, is that Sartre follows Nietzsche in his emphasis on the responsibility – in the absence of God – to choose values and live by them. The particular twist that Sartre gives to this process is that we act first and display our values through that action. We do not select who we want to be and then try to live up to it (that would lead to bad faith) but we shape ourselves, and thereby reveal our values: we are as we act. And that is what constitutes the seriousness of existentialist ethics; it is all down to us, there is no eternal set of values, no blueprint in the form of an ideal 'essence' of humankind to guide us.

Values and partridges

Throughout our study of existentialism so far, we have encountered the issue of values. From Nietzsche to Sartre, it has been clear that values are not discovered 'out there' in any scientific analysis of the world, but are created by an act of will. We have choices to make and a freedom and responsibility that we cannot escape; we decide what we are for, since the world provides us with no predetermined essence.

Now one of the problems with this is that, if values are created rather than discovered, it is difficult to see how people can feel committed to *shared* values. After all, even if people clearly admit to having the same values, their commitment to them is entirely personal, and may be revised at any time.

It is clear that, for Sartre, values are not discovered in isolation but in action. He uses a wonderful analogy for this, describing values as springing up ahead of us 'like partridges' (*Being and Nothingness*, p. 62). Thus, as we move forward through life, values and commitments suddenly appear before us, because of the direction in which we have chosen to walk.

But his choice of that analogy poses a problem. If I am out walking in the countryside, I do not *create* the birds I am about to scare out of the undergrowth, I discover them. It would be just as logical therefore to claim that you are *discovering* values *in* action, rather than *creating* values *by* action. As Sartre presents it, however, it is my freedom that determines how I act, and my approval or otherwise of what I discover that gives rise to value. But this begs the question: 'Why does this particular situation gain my indignation or admiration?' Why is it that the partridge springs up at this particular point? And might I want to claim that it would similarly spring up for anyone who freely chose to walk to that particular spot?

Sartre uses his visual images in order to 'show' his existential analysis, indeed, that is a key feature of the way he argues in *Being and Nothingness*. On this occasion, however, his image is ambiguous, and we are therefore entitled to entertain the possibility that values make themselves known to us because we discover them, rather than create them.

Sartre himself was scathing of 'respectable' morality and values:

> *The bourgeois who call themselves 'respectable citizens' do not become respectable as the result of contemplating moral values. Rather from the moment of their arising in the world they are thrown into a pattern of behaviour the meaning of which is respectability. Thus respectability acquires a being; it is not put into question. Values are sown on my path as thousands of little real demands, like the signs which order us to keep off the grass.*
>
> *Being and Nothingness* (p. 62)

To sink into respectability, to do what is expected, is to live in bad faith. To be authentic, to be a true existentialist, we should boldly forge our own values and lifestyle, constructing our own morality.

The problem with such existential morality is that, since there is no external value beyond what one creates through one's own commitments, the power of commitment becomes its own moral justification. (Nietzsche's advice was: 'Choose your own perspective, but live with the knowledge that such a perspective has no warrant but that of your will.') Yet, if that is so, how can we ever get a perspective from which to say what we all know, namely that people can sometimes be sincerely wrong and unwisely committed? How, if at all, can we get outside our own commitment and perspective? But that question takes us into the world of post-modernism...

The book that never was

At the end of *Being and Nothingness* (p. 645), Sartre makes clear the relationship between his ontology (the study or being) and ethics:

> **Ontology itself can not formulate ethical precepts. It is concerned solely with what is, and we can not possibly derive imperatives from ontology's indicatives. It does, however, allow us to catch a glimpse of what sort of ethics will assume its responsibilities when confronted with a human reality in situation.**

In other words, all that he has explored so far sets the scene for a study of ethics. In fact, right at the end of the book, exploring questions of freedom, choice and bad faith, he concludes:

> **All these questions, which refer us to a pure and not an accessory (or impure) reflection, can find their reply only on the ethical plane. We shall devote to them a future work.**

In fact, that 'future work' was never written. All we have, in terms of a work specifically on ethics, is his *Notebooks for an Ethics*, written in 1947/8, along with the hints at a form of Kantian ethics, given briefly in his 'Existentialism is a Humanism' lecture.

One problem with existentialist ethics is that it appears to be centred on the individual, rather than on a concern for the welfare of all. Thus, for example, Iris Murdoch (in *The Sovereignty of Good*, p. 47) opposes existentialist ethics on the grounds that morality requires unselfishness, whereas she thinks that existentialism is always ego-bound. But key existentialist thinkers, including Sartre himself, themselves struggled with the social dimension. Thus, in *Existentialism and Humanism*, Sartre argues that one should strive not just for one's own freedom but for the freedom of all, and Jaspers feared that the value of philosophy would be lost if it remained hidden in the world of personal communication rather than engaging in the crucial issues of the day.

Nevertheless, there is a fundamental difference in approach between those (like Murdoch) who take a basically Platonic view of eternal values, and the values on which existential thought is based. Foundational values are not (for the existentialist) objectively given, they are created. We do not discover them, we create them. But in that case, what grounds do you have for prescribing such values to others, which is what moral claims appear to be doing?

If it is to escape accusations of being egocentric and self-indulgent, existentialism needs to link its view of authenticity to the general good of society. This is what Sartre attempted to do in his famous 1945 lecture, showing that existentialism stood within a genuinely humanist tradition.

The degree to which Sartre succeeded in that attempt to link his existentialism to traditional humanism is a matter of debate, not least because he himself was later to regret the position he took at that time. What we do know, however, is that existentialism insists that we are responsible for constructing and taking responsibility for our values and the commitments they reflect.

Far from being nihilist, existentialists take commitments seriously, selecting values and living by them. They refuse conform to established norms simply because they do not want to become part of the impersonal world of the 'in-itself'.

Lawrence of Arabia: an existentialist hero?

In her essay *The Ethics of Ambiguity* (*Pour une morale de l'ambiguïté*, 1948) Simone de Beauvoir acclaimed a hidden

(Contd)

existentialist hero: T.E. Lawrence, 'Lawrence of Arabia'. Her choice of such a romantic man of action – the legendary English scholar–soldier who led the Arab revolt against the Turks in the First World War and related his experiences in *The Seven Pillars of Wisdom* (1926) – was not as odd as it might at first seem. Existentialists always revered men of action, at least in theory, and Lawrence was an unusually complex, intelligent and self-torturing man. The British colonel was also much admired by Sartre and by Simone Weil (1909–43), the heterodox Christian mystic and political radical, for the way he set out to change the world while never losing his capacity to feel the doubt and *angoisse* of an existentialist. Camus' heroic doctor Bernard Rieux in his novel *The Plague* (*La Peste*), who battles to save the infected city, displays the same typical mixture of doubt, anguish and determination.

The ethics of ambiguity

Ontology itself can not formulate ethical precepts. It is concerned solely with what is, and we can not possibly derive imperatives from ontology's indicatives.

Sartre, *Being and Nothingness* (p. 645)

Clearly, there is always going to be a problem (referred to in philosophy as the 'naturalistic fallacy') of moving from 'is' to 'ought', but if existentialism describes what it is to be a human being, embedded in the world and yet always transcending it, that view of humankind is bound to have implications for how people understand themselves, and how they evaluate action. It was highlighted by the idea of authentic and inauthentic existence – so that, if existentialism cannot (and absolutely will not!) tell you what you ought to do, it will at least point out when you are being intellectually dishonest, or self-deceiving.

On the one hand existentialists see people as meaning-giving, free individuals who care nothing for what society expects or regards as the norm – a view that is reinforced by the popular image of the existentialist lifestyle. On the other, they want to affirm that people are subject to the look of others, that they live in society. This is the 'ambiguity' in existence to which both Merleau Ponty and de Beauvoir refer.

In *The Ethics of Ambiguity* (1947) de Beauvoir presents an ethics that works within the general parameters of Sartrean existentialism, but it is given a more political and less individualist slant than in the work of Sartre himself.

We need to focus here on the nature of the ambiguity described by de Beauvoir. On the one hand, you have the human desire for freedom, for self-affirmation, for escaping social pressures to conform – all of those features that made existentialism so popular. On the other hand, every individual is located in a physical, social and political environment, with his or her life determined to a considerable extent by factors that are not within his or her control.

So any ethical argument must recognize this ambiguity, that one may be at one and the same time free, and yet constrained. To accept only the constraint is to kill off all freedom and live in bad faith; to accept only freedom is to be naïvely unrealistic and escapist.

It is also important to recognize that, for de Beauvoir, other people do not necessarily limit your own freedom but may actually be the means of making freedom possible. And freedom, of course, is not seen simply in terms of doing whatever you wish – that would be quite naïve – but in having a sense of a future in which one might freely choose between possibilities. And that may require a social movement rather than simply an individual vision.

Her view of ethics takes into account the social changes of the past; it is not simply an ethics of a moment of free existential decision.

It also recognizes that one's own freedom may only be exercised in the context of the freedom of others – and indeed of a changed social situation in which, for example, an oppressed group can affirm themselves. And there will always be ways in which oppressors try to justify their oppression, perhaps in terms of the essence or natural qualities of the group whom they wish to keep in place. To liberate individuals in such a situation, it is necessary to change society.

Insight

Examples of this might be the anti-apartheid movement in South Africa and the civil rights movement in the southern states of the USA. The freedom of the individual becomes possible only in a social and political context.

But whatever some of its critics might claim, existentialism is not simply focused on the individual. When he launched his periodical *Les Temps Moderne* in 1945, Sartre saw it as a vehicle not just for liberating individuals, but also for changing society, and this is seen also in the work of de Beauvoir, Marcel, Jaspers and Merleau-Ponty. But the issue of how existentialism relates to social change brings us to another major issue: the relationship between existentialism and Marxism.

A Marxist view?

One of the most curious features of Sartre's thought is how rapidly his existentialism was subsumed within his commitment to Marxism. In the question and answer session, printed in *Existentialism and Humanism* as the responses to Sartre's popular lecture in 1945, one of the questioners argued that the existentialist, like the liberal, considers man in general, rather than considering what the events require, and that the only progressive position is given in Marxism. He went on to claim that 'Marxism alone states the real problems of the age' (p. 83). Sartre, in response, did not answer directly nor did he define the relationship between existentialism and Marxism. But he agreed with his questioner in that 'each epoch develops according to dialectical laws, and men depend upon their epoch and not upon human nature' (p. 91). Clearly, for Sartre, this was not the time to develop a careful argument about the relationship between existential free choice and the conditions of the epoch under which people live.

For left-wing rebels, however, existentialism and Marxism appeared to hold together very conveniently – with the former determining most personal choices and the latter being applicable to the global view and class consciousness. But there is a fundamental difference between Marxist ethics and those espoused by existentialism. For Marx, social and political change is brought about by the material means of sustaining life, by the social and class structures, and by the production and distribution of goods and services. People behave according to their place within an overall materialist **dialectic** – a view that he developed from Hegel's view of social and cultural change.

Hegel, Marx and Sartre have one absolutely fundamental thing in common – that humankind is embedded in the physical world. But for Hegel, people follow the 'spirit of the age' and for Marx they act as a member of a social class. How is that compatible with existentialism? After all, a key feature of Heidegger's work is that one should not conform to the masks that society offers, and Sartre insists on the freedom of the 'for-itself' not to become (and to believe oneself to be) an object, an 'in-itself'. But a key feature of Marxism is that one acts within one's class, as a member of the bourgeoisie or proletariat.

Insight

A fundamental question here: How can you act as a member of a class and not see yourself as taking on a role, adopting a mask, or accepting yourself as an 'in-itself', governed by the social forces that shape the movement towards an eventual dictatorship of the proletariat? Where is human freedom in the inevitable march of history?

The Paris Hegelians and *The End of History*

Despite Kierkegaard and Nietzsche's rejection of Hegel, his thought influenced French philosophy via two outstanding Hegelian teachers in mid-twentieth-century Paris: Alexandre Koyré (1892–1964) and his heir Alexandre Kojève (1902–68). Both were Russian émigrés who had fled the Bolshevik Revolution yet had Marxist sympathies. Some of the students attracted to their classes, especially Kojève's, later became very important in French political and intellectual life: the philosophers Merleau-Ponty, de Beauvoir and Jacques Lacan; the surrealist writers André Breton and Raymond Queneau; and Georges Batailles, both a philosopher and a surrealist. What attracted the French to Hegel was not his lofty universal idealism which so appealed to northern Europe, but his theory of the evolution of power relationships between the upper and lower classes (which he described, as did Nietzsche, by an analogy with a 'master–slave' relationship) as the dialectic driving forward a universal historical process towards final reconciliation and unity. Giving Hegel's thinking a Marxist spin, Kojève synthesized it with Heidegger's ontology in *Being and Time* to create a historicized form of existentialism. He offered a vision of History in which humanity seizes its freedom to recreate the world while pursuing its desires, driving History towards its end or goal. Kojève's most famous theory, the End of History, was later popularized by the American academic Francis Fukuyama in his unexpected bestseller *The End of History and the Last Man* (1992). After the fall of the Berlin Wall and the Soviet empire, Fukuyama saw History ending happily with the global triumph of a liberal capitalism that would satisfy all human aspirations. If Fukuyama's theory seems less plausible than it did 18 years ago, Kojève's more nuanced ideas have stood the test of time better. Through Koyré and Kojève, Hegel became the first of 'the three Hs' – along with Husserl and Heidegger – to exert a deep influence on Sartre and other existentialists.

In 1957, Sartre published a short piece on Marxism and existentialism which later, as 'Question of Method', became the introduction to his major work *The Critique of Dialectical Reason* (1960). What he argues there is that every era has its own dominant philosophy, and for his time it was Marxism. Existentialism cannot be a rival to this, and so becomes merely an ideology that may contribute to Marxist thought but cannot contradict it.

But while he describes existentialism as a 'parasitical system living on the margin of Knowledge', and Marxism as the 'unsurpassable framework of knowledge', he acknowledges the danger that Marxism may become dehumanized, and hopes that existentialism will be able to prevent that happening. Indeed, he argues that, when Marxism takes on the human dimension, there will be no more need for a separate philosophy of existentialism.

But there was never a consensus view on this among existentialist thinkers. It led to bitter ruptures between Sartre and his fellow thinkers Camus and (particularly) Merleau-Ponty, who offers this comment:

> **There was exploitation long before there were revolutionaries. Nor is it always in periods of economic difficulty that the working class movement makes headway. Revolt is, then, not an outcome of objective conditions, but it is rather the decision taken by the worker to will revolution that makes a proletarian of him.** The evaluation of the present operates through one's free project for the future.
>
> *The Phenomenology of Perception* (p. 443)

If dialectical materialism is right, then it is exactly the material conditions that determine the class struggle. But what Merleau-Ponty argues is that those material conditions do not determine what happens, because that can only happen when people evaluate those conditions in the light of their hopes for the future and then decide on action.

Further discussion of these issues takes us beyond the scope of this book, but it does raise a serious question about whether existentialism provides a sufficient guide for dealing with the world of human society. If Heidegger, having developed his view of the individual in *Being and Time* can then (albeit briefly) be tempted by the challenge of national socialism, and if Sartre, having extolled the virtue of non-conformity, can be committed to the cause of communism under Stalin, one has to question how well existentialist ethics relates to the wider questions of political commitment.

10 THINGS TO REMEMBER

1 *Existentialism sees social conformity as threatening individual authenticity.*

2 *Freedom is experienced as real, even if, seen as 'objects', we appear to be determined by circumstances.*

3 *I am free to choose, but not necessarily to achieve what I want.*

4 *Being free, we are without excuse and must take full responsibility for our actions.*

5 *In choosing freedom and values for ourselves, we do so for everyone.*

6 *We cannot blame our circumstances for what we choose to do.*

7 *We construct morality and choose values.*

8 *We experience an ambiguity of experiencing freedom and yet being constrained by circumstances.*

9 *De Beauvoir and others see individual liberation as requiring a change in social structures.*

10 *Sartre thought existentialism could humanize Marxism.*

7

The individual, art and society

In this chapter you will learn:
- *that existentialist thinking influenced post-war art and atrists*
- *that existentialists mingled with and knew many avant-grade artists*
- *that ideas of commitment concerned artists as well as thinkers*

Existentialists never had or wanted to have an ivory tower of any sort, academic or romantic. They were happy to live in the centre of modern cities, most notably in Paris, where they frequented street cafés abuzz with the latest ideas. Sartre called the magazine he founded in 1945 *Les Temps Modernes*. The title referred to Charlie Chaplin's satirical film *Modern Times* of 1936 that had attacked the modern industrial world. For Sartre it indicated on the contrary a determined acceptance of modernity. As philosophers go, existentialists were unusually aware of, and influenced by, the latest trends in society and the arts. The influence ran both ways. Existentialism affected the art of post-war Paris more than any other philosophical school has done. This was partly due to the exceptional atmosphere of Paris at the time.

When existentialism emerged in Paris in the 1940s, the city had been the centre of modern art for almost a century, home to successive radical movements: realism, Impressionism, Post-Impressionism, cubism, Fauvism and surrealism. It had become famed as the City of Light, attracting artists, writers and bohemians from across the world. (The term *bohemian* itself comes from *Scènes de la Vie de Bohème* of 1849 by Henri Murger, a writer who lived a true bohemian's life, dying in abject poverty. Puccini's famous opera *La Bohème* of 1896 was based on Murger's book.) Paris had also long been a beacon of political, social and intellectual freedom to people fleeing persecution of any sort. This reputation revived, albeit fragilely, after 1945. The 'School of Paris', the pre-war group of foreign artists that had included Chagall and Miró, was proudly re-established.

The phenomenon of the modern art dealer, crucial both to the success of individual artists and of the whole avant-garde, had also emerged first in Paris. Paul Durand-Ruel, the pioneer among such dealers, risked his fortune in supporting the Impressionists for years before they had real commercial success. He bought 20 canvases by Edouard Manet in 1872 alone, and bravely exhibited numerous paintings by Claude Monet in New York in 1885 despite the artist's own reservations about the venture. (Keen American buyers of these works saved Durand-Ruel from financial ruin.) Ambroise Vollard similarly encouraged avant-garde art, holding the first one-man exhibition of Paul Cézanne, the greatest Post-Impressionist, in 1895, Picasso's first solo show in 1901 and Henri Matisse's in 1904. Daniel-Henri Kahnweiler continued this vital process, patiently nurturing the fortunes of leading cubists such as Picasso, Juan Gris and Georges Braque.

After 1945 New York steadily displaced Paris as the capital of the visual arts, but this was not at once apparent either in France or abroad. Foreign artists and writers – among them the Swiss-born sculptor and painter Alberto Giacometti (1901–66) and the Irish-born Samuel Beckett – still regarded Paris as their obvious home. It was still a city of unparalleled allure. The years after 1945 saw, besides the emergence of existentialism, the rebirth of French fashion (Dior's romantic New Look) and of French cinema (Jacques Tati's satirical films about modern society featuring Monsieur Hulot). Both, if typically French in their charm, were traditional, even nostalgic in their outlook.

In the visual arts, however, a truly novel savagery and apparent ugliness emerged, *art brut* (literally: 'crude' or 'raw art'), involving materials like sand and great impasto daubs of paint. Jean Dubuffet, an artist and writer who had his first one-man exhibition in 1945, was the most articulate of its practitioners. 'The idea that there are beautiful objects and ugly objects, people blessed with beauty and others without it, surely rests only on convention – it's nonsense,' he wrote. 'I declare such conventions diseased…. People notice that I aim to sweep away everything that we have taught to think unquestioningly beautiful and graceful, but they overlook my efforts to substitute another, greater beauty, covering every being and object, including the most despised... I want people to look on my work as an attempt to rehabilitate scorned values... I am convinced that any table can for each of us be a landscape as inexhaustible as the whole Andes range.'

Insight

Only an art like Dubuffet's seemed to the existentialists to match the age that had begun in 1945, the age of Auschwitz and Hiroshima. But while unusually eloquent, Dubuffet was merely one among many French artist–propagandists.

Authentic experience: artists, writers and musicians

Most philosophers have tended to shy away from artists and writers. Whatever their own tastes in the creative arts, logical thinkers have often considered actual artists and poets unreliable bohemians. Not so the existentialists. The emaciated 'stick-like' figures of Alberto Giacometti quiver with a tension and anguish which was quickly recognized as typically existentialist. Sartre first met Giacometti in 1939 just as the artist was beginning to evolve his utterly original style after going through a surrealist phase.

For existentialism, a philosophy that called on human beings to define themselves through their actions, artistic creativity was always supremely important. Sartre saw in the artist who produces original work from nothing a paradigm of authentic human existence. 'In life a man commits himself, draws his own portrait and there is nothing but that portrait', he wrote. 'As everyone knows, there are no aesthetic values *a priori*... no one can tell what a painting tomorrow will be like.' This emphasis on the new-created – of which there can be no prior (*a priori*) knowledge, and so no aesthetic rules – underlay much of existentialism's appeal to avant-garde artists.

Insight

Clearly, existence precedes essence applies to art as much as to human reality; in art, as in life, we are challenged to create our own aesthetic values.

Well before Sartre began extolling his contemporaries in the 1940s, he had been interested in modernism. He saw its struggles as complementing his own literary and philosophical efforts, aptly for a thinker who spent most of his life in Paris. At the beginning of the twentieth century the cubists' radical fracturing of form had led to the destruction of single-viewpoint linear 'mathematical' perspective. Linear perspective had underpinned all Western art since the fifteenth-century Renaissance, giving it the seemingly objective assurance that helped make Western art unmistakeably 'Western'. But from now on it was possible, even required, for artists to depict objects from multiple viewpoints, as if seen simultaneously from several angles, as if there were no 'correct' way of looking at anything. Each artist could – must – create the visual world afresh.

This revolution, initiated by Picasso and Braque following in Cézanne's footsteps, was a response to perceived artistic, not intellectual, problems and long predated existentialism. *Les Demoiselles d'Avignon* (or *The Brothel*, as Picasso candidly first called it) the prototypical cubist work, was painted in 1907, although Picasso did not exhibit it in public until 1916, aware of its explosive potential. It is still startling today, as much for its savage energy and novel ugliness inspired by non-European art as for its disregard of linear perspective. More than any other work, it signalled the advent of a new aesthetics.

Philosophers, artists, actors...

The friendship of Picasso with Sartre and de Beauvoir reveals how closely the existentialists could become involved with the arts. It began during the German occupation of Paris (1940–4), when all three were effectively trapped in the city. The two writers, along with Dora Maar, one of Picasso's mistresses, acted in the clandestine first performance of the painter's play *Desire Caught by the Tail* (*Désir Attrapé par la Queue*) in early 1944. Camus directed this surrealistic rarity in Picasso's freezing studio in the rue des Grands-Augustins. It proved a one-off: Picasso never wrote another play and the philosophers did not pursue stage careers, returning to their intellectual pursuits. Yet some felt there had been a paradoxical liberty under the Nazis which forced on all French people a trial of their good (or bad) faith. Sartre himself wrote after the liberation in August 1944: 'We were never so free as under the German occupation... each thought was a conquest. As an all-powerful police sought to silence us, each word became as valuable as a declaration of principle. As we were pursued, each gesture had the weight of an engagement.' (*La République du Silence, Les Lettres Françaises*, 1944)

The new aesthetics was evident in the other arts. T.S. Eliot, who lived for a time in Paris, pioneered 'free verse', most famously in *The Waste Land* (1922), often considered the twentieth-century's archetypal poem. 'Free prose' was probably pioneered by Gertrude Stein, another American resident in Paris who wrote maddeningly repetitive prose, but its time genius was James Joyce, an Irish writer, also living in Paris after 1918. Joyce's bewildering, exhilarating polyphonic novel *Ulysses* of 1922 broke all rules, including those on obscenity. (For these reasons the novel could not be published in the Irish Republic for more than 40 years.)

From now on chronological narrative, the backbone of the nineteenth-century novel, seemed incidental, almost redundant. In Marcel Proust's immense novel *In Search of Lost Time*

(*A la Recherche du Temps Perdu*, 1909–22), time itself dissolves to become a mirror-like maze through which the narrator wanders, half in entranced reverie, half in caustic observation.

A similar revolution shattered the world of classical music. The primitive pulsations of Stravinsky's ballet *The Rite of Spring (Le Sacré du Printemps)*, premiered in Paris in 1913, marked a crucial change in Western music, from all-resolving final harmony to spiky, savagely driving rhythm. Traditional musical form could never be the same again. If a lot of classical music did not continue far in this direction, jazz, which arrived in Paris from the USA in the 1920s, certainly did. Modernism, while elitist in its disdain for public opinion, was relentless in its attack on old hierarchies.

Insight

This artistic 'revaluation of all values' (Nietzsche's words) presaged the total psychological and social uprooting that the two world wars confirmed in politics. By 1945 a process that had started gently with the Impressionists – who chose to paint scenes of everyday life, such as streets, river banks and domestic interiors, rather than officially favoured grand historical or religious subjects – was producing an art of strident *angoisse* well suited to existentialism. If the novels by Sartre, Camus and de Beauvoir proved conventional enough in narrative form, their contents were truly radical, exciting readers around the world. As de Beauvoir wrote, 'France, having become a second class power, defended itself by glorifying its exports, Fashion and Literature.'

Cézanne, master of anxiety

The years immediately after 1945 saw renewed admiration for Paul Cézanne among the avant-garde in Paris. This might seem a little odd for a painter who had by then been dead for nearly 40 years. Cézanne had died in 1906 aged 68 and his posthumous fame had steadily grown until he was widely regarded as the greatest artist of his age. In Cézanne's wonderful landscapes of Mont Ste-Victoire or his still lifes of apples and bottles, he seemed to have grasped the very essence of objects, be they mountains or fruits, painting form with a passionate lucidity.

Yet Cézanne's time-defying, quasi-geometrical art – seeing in nature 'the cylinder, the sphere, the cone' as he put it – was achieved only at huge personal cost and repeated professional disappointments. Looked at again, his apples, tables and bottles almost burst from their canvases with tension and stress; the sharp rocks of his Provençal mountains jut out restlessly as if into a fourth dimension. Acute personal nervousness underlies all his monumental paintings, not just his 'morbid' early works. It was this *angoisse* (anguish) which appealed to the existentialists, who acclaimed the painter as a suffering hero of the easel precisely because of his neuroses.

In 'Cézanne's Doubt' (*La doute de Cézanne*), an article of December 1945, Merleau-Ponty hailed Cézanne as a proto-existentialist. 'If painting was his world and his existence, anxiety was the basis of his character', wrote Merleau-Ponty, detecting in Cézanne's art 'a morbidity... schizophrenia... a flight from the world of humanity.' To Merleau-Ponty, at least at this stage in his thinking, as well as to other existentialists, such morbidity was potentially fruitful, for 'there is a connection between the schizoid constitution and Cézanne's work because his work reveals a metaphysical sense of his illness. If we regard schizophrenia as a state of mind in which the world is reduced to the sum of all its physical experiences but as if frozen, as a suspension of expressive values, then [mental] illness, in Cézanne's case, is no longer just absurd and ill-fated but opens up valid possibilities for all human existence.'

Merleau-Ponty's analysis – whether or not accurate about Cézanne, who if morbidly shy was never considered mentally ill – echoed Freud's famous psychoanalysis of Leonardo da Vinci. (This itself is now known to be flawed owing to a then common fallacy about Leonardo's infancy, but it was admired at the time.) The immediate heirs of Cézanne were the cubists, who carried his geometrical revolution to its conclusion.

Existentialist artists

From cubism a convoluted line runs – with a detour via Dadaism, that most nihilist of movements, and surrealism, the most flamboyant – to *art brut*. This school of art emerged at the same time, and as a response to the same circumstances, as existentialism. 'Raw art' was supposedly best made by psychotics – prisoners and others on society's extreme fringes – but in reality its practitioners soon became part of the art world. The actual term was coined by Dubuffet, who claimed that such art 'sprang from pure invention and was in no way based, as cultural art constantly is, on chameleon or parrot-like processes'. Instead it reveals an aggressive originality that everyone possesses but which is too often stifled by education and social constraints.

Insight

Dubuffet believed that art should seek for the roots of mental activity, where 'thought is close to birth'. After reading Sartre's novel *Nausea* he declared, 'I haven't quite understood what existentialism actually is… But I feel and declare myself warmly existentialist.' His often grotesque paintings depicting street life and more abstract themes and his method of plastering his canvases with raw materials such as sand and plaster divided opinion then and to this day.

Bram van Velde (1895–1981), a Dutch-born artist who arrived in Paris in 1936 to fall deeply under Picasso's influence, wrote in 1948: 'Only those who are sick can be artists. It is their suffering which drives them to do the things that restore meaning to the world. The sensitive man or artist can only be sick in our civilized life filled with lies…Painting is man confronting catastrophe… I paint my misery.' Van Velde had no commercial success despite praise from Samuel Beckett, which may in part explain his misery.

Misérabiliste was the name of the style associated with Dubuffet and especially with Francis Gruber (1912–48), a French artist who died of TB. Gruber's mature style exudes a wintry melancholy, whether his subject is a nude, still life or landscape. Typical is *Job*, painted in 1944 and exhibited at the Salon d'Automne (the key annual exhibition) that year. Depicting the Old Testament character sorely tested by God, Gruber's Job, seated gaunt and nude on a stool in silent contemplation, symbolized the existentialist despair of the oppressed people of Paris, who yet retained their ultimate faith in their liberation. Gruber was from the start a politically committed painter, a Communist at a time when most existentialists were not.

Sartre championed Wols as the purest example of an existentialist artist, however. Wols was the pseudonym of the German-born Alfred Schulze (1913–51), who had studied at the Bauhaus, the modernist seminary in Weimar Germany, before moving to France in 1932 to escape the Nazis. After working initially as a photographer, he had his first solo show as a painter in December 1945. Soon he was producing highly original abstract works that rivalled, albeit on a smaller scale, those of contemporary American abstract expressionists. Despite Sartre's support, Wols lived in abject poverty, a situation he seemed almost to relish.

Sartre, who had first met Wols in 1945, recalled that he was 'bald with a bottle and a beggar's slouch...at 33 one would have thought him 50, had it not been for the youthful sadness in his eyes. Everyone thought that he would not make old bones. In the end his friends had to carry him in the evening to the Rhumerie Martinique [a bar] and bring him back in the middle of the night, a little more dead each day, a little more visionary.' Wols illustrated several of Sartre's books – usually in drypoint (black and white engraving on copper) – with designs of a savagery that thrilled the philosopher.

The artist most intimately connected with the existentialists themselves was the sculptor Alberto Giacometti, who made numerous portraits of de Beauvoir. Sartre in *The Search for the Absolute*, his introduction to the New York exhibition of 1948 that finally established Giacometti's reputation, hailed him as the age's greatest artist. He declared that Giacometti's only true rivals were the Palaeolithic artists of Altamira, not any twentieth-century contemporaries. (On visiting these famous cave paintings in northern Spain earlier, Picasso had said: 'After Altamira, all is decadence'.) Sartre himself wrote: 'After 3,000 [sic] years, the task of Giacometti and of contemporary sculptors is not to enrich the galleries with new works, but to prove that sculpture itself is still possible... there is a definite goal to be attained, a single problem to be solved: how to mould a man in stone without petrifying him.'

Insight

Sartre's view of Giacometti as the artist of despair and apostle of neo-Palaeolithic primitivism was widely shared. To an art critic in New York who saw his 1948 exhibition, Giacometti's figures were 'fugitives from Dachau', the Nazi concentration camp. While Giacometti rejected the more obvious interpretations of his work, there was a constant exchange of ideas between the artist and the intellectuals who visited his studio in Montparnasse.

Merleau-Ponty in his 1961 essay *Eye and Mind* asserted that Giacometti's understanding of 'resemblance' was close to his own phenomenological approach. 'Resemblance is the result of perception, not its origin,' he wrote. Merleau-Ponty differentiated between *habitual* perception, based on knowledge accumulated over time, and *authentic* perception which, like the vision of a newborn child, precedes knowledge. Giacometti frequently used the same models – often members of his family – for his emaciated figures, but he claimed to look at them afresh each time. He said of his brother Diego Giacometti: 'He has posed ten thousand times for me, but the next time he poses I won't recognize him.'

Despite ever-growing success – in 1962 he won the grand prize for sculpture at the Venice Biennale – Giacometti led a frugal, even ascetic existence, reputedly living off black coffee and hard-boiled eggs. As de Beauvoir later said of him: 'Success, fame, money – Giacometti was indifferent to them all.'

A similar, genuinely bohemian indifference was exhibited by jazz musicians such as Boris Vian, who was also a poet, satirist, musician and actor. In the late 1940s Vian, along with singers like Juliette Gréco (born 1927), used to perform in the small cellar night-clubs of Saint-Germain-des-Prés on the Left Bank, often underneath the very cafés where Sartre and company were debating. Jazz, after being banned under the German occupation, still seemed alluringly new. This milieu attracted among others the American writer James Baldwin, who found in it an escape from the racism and homophobia then prevalent in the USA. (A different, jaundiced view of French intellectual life came from the waspish American playwright Truman Capote. He described Sartre as 'wall-eyed, pipe-sucking, pasty-faced' and de Beauvoir as a 'spinsterish moll', the two 'propped up in a corner like an abandoned pair of ventriloquist's dolls.')

Politics, art and commitment

These artistic and intellectual events unfolded in a world that had not yet begun to recover from the Second World War. Across Europe tens of millions of people were starving or homeless; France itself was half-ruined. Food rationing was re-imposed at even lower rates – the butter ration, for example, was *cut* in 1945 from 175 grams to 100 grams per month. Fuel also was in short supply in a series of bitter winters.

Even worse was the psychological shock of seeing films of the newly-opened concentration camps in Germany. When spectral French survivors from these arrived at the Gare de l'Est, the crowds waiting to welcome them dissolved into tears. 'The Europe of bombed-out ghost towns is no more ravaged than the idea that Europe has made of humanity,' wrote André Malraux, the novelist and Resistance fighter. A new ethic, a new humanism, was needed. With prophetic splendour Sartre rose to the challenge in his lecture 'Existentialism is a Humanism' ('*L'Existentialisme est une Humanisme*') in 1945. But his emphasis on personal responsibility soon risked seeming irrelevant or outdated.

Following the euphoria of national unity at the Liberation in the summer of 1944, rooted divisions re-emerged between the powerful French Communist party, taking its orders direct from Stalinist Moscow, and most other French people. Despite this the existentialists initially tried to retain some intellectual and ideological independence. Then in 1947 the Communists quit the post-war coalition government and began to organize damagingly disruptive strikes, at the same time supporting Soviet expansion around the world. In 1948 the blockade of Berlin, when Soviet attempts to force the Allies out of Berlin were countered by a massive airlift, signalled the onset of the Cold War proper. It became increasingly hard for anyone in public life to remain uncommitted politically.

Picasso had openly joined the French Communist Party in late 1944. (He had not been a Communist when he had supported the beleaguered Spanish Republic in 1937 by painting *Guernica*, his famous work depicting the disasters of war.) This was not an opportunistic move – Picasso risked alienating potential wealthy American buyers by such a public gesture – but it gave him a sense of belonging to a larger community than fellow artists could provide. (He could never revisit his native Spain under Franco's dictatorship, which was to outlast him.) Along with the physicist Frédéric Joliot-Curie, the painter Fernand Léger, the writer Louis Aragon and the actress Simone Signoret, he was henceforth enrolled in a Communist phalanx of intellectual-cum-artistic celebrities.

Yet it was a paradoxical move aesthetically. Picasso's main art of the time, such as *The Charnel House* (1945) was in a semi-abstract style recalling *Guernica*. This was far removed from the Socialist realist style that the Communists usually demanded. Much closer to the official Party line in the arts was Boris Taslitzky's *The Small Camp, Buchenwald* exhibited next to Picasso's work at the Musée Nationale d'Art Moderne in 1946. Taslitzky, who had risked his life making drawings as a prisoner inside the concentration camp, depicted Buchenwald's horrors in a realist style that recalled Géricault's *Raft of the Medusa* (1819). This earlier famous work with a political message had been found shocking at first but then had become an icon of French art. Taslitzky's huge canvas was likewise soon bought for the nation.

Taslitzky had been a member of the Communist Party since 1936 and would remain a devout Communist until his death at the age of 94 in 2005. Arguments arose in late 1946 about whether his art had greater 'authenticity' than that of Picasso, the new convert to Communism, as well as about their different styles. Taslitzky had links with Giacometti and especially with Gruber, whose tortured work, also in realist style, seemed to epitomize the existentialist predicament. Gruber, however, died in 1948, although he remained a substantial influence on artists of the 1950s.

Koestler, Sartre and de Beauvoir

Darkness at Noon, the first novel to reveal the full horrors of Stalinism as seen by a senior Communist Party member, was published as *Le Zero et L'Infini* in France 1946. Its great popularity – it quickly sold 400,000 copies – infuriated the Communists. The author was Arthur Koestler, Hungarian-born but by then living in Britain. Koestler had been a keen Communist in the 1930s. Then experience of Stalinism during the Spanish Civil War turned him into one of Communism's fiercest critics. In 1946 Koestler visited Paris and met Sartre. The two very different men exchanged views for a while, despite disagreements from the start. 'I don't believe that my point of view is superior to yours, or yours to mine,' Sartre wrote magnanimously, but the two were never real friends. (Nor did the one-night stand that de Beauvoir had with Koestler lead to anything. Both were famously promiscuous.) Later, as Sartre moved ever closer to Communism while Koestler became more interested in science and the paranormal, the gulf between the existentialists and him became unbridgeable.

Where did this artistic debate leave the existentialists? The answer was: at times in a quandary, looking disunited. Merleau-Ponty, who as joint editor with Sartre of *Les Temps Modernes* was a noted public figure, in late 1947 wrote *Humanism and Terror: Essays on the Communist Problem*. In these pieces he tried to justify the infamous show trials of the 1930s – when many old Communists had been killed on patently trumped up charges – and the general Stalinist terror as a necessary part of the greater good that resulted from the Communist revolution. Only Marxism offered humanity any hope within the grand schema of History. In such deeply political circumstances, individual responsibility is much diminished. (Later, Merleau-Ponty altered his views on Communism sharply.)

Yet other existentialists at the time, notably Sartre, insisted on the individual's absolute and involuntary freedom – 'We are condemned to be free', as he put it – and each person's concomitant 'absolute responsibility'. The clash between these two viewpoints did not, however, at this stage become crucial. The whole of Sartre's writings and the post-war art of Giacometti, Dubuffet and others formed an important conjunction of philosophy and art, the one illuminating and inspiring the other in a way seldom seen.

Left brain, right brain: philosophy versus the arts

Findings of neuroscience have confirmed what many have long suspected: the sometimes seemingly insurmountable gulf between the intellect and the emotions is based on biology. Philosophy, like maths and our tax returns, we mostly do with the left rational logical half of the brain; we do the arts, from poetry to painting, with the right intuitive non-logical half. If we are left-handed, these positions may be reversed – much depends on the individual. (Of course mathematicians use their right brains just as artists at times use their left, but the formula seems to hold true overall.) This division has a long history in philosophy.

Plato, although he wrote poetry when young and then dialogues of superb literary merit, distrusted all forms of art from painting to poetry. He preferred the purity of mathematics. In *Republic,* his central work, he advised expelling poets and artists from his ideal state for telling misleading if bewitching lies. His greatest pupil Aristotle took a more positive view, however, considering drama's fictional truth superior to that of history because it could penetrate deeper into men's hearts and motives. The Neoplatonist philosopher Plotinus (CE 204–70) wrote an ecstatic essay *On Beauty* in which he claimed that art could give us intimations of the divine reality behind the flux of life. Plotinus anticipated some of the aesthetic views of Immanuel Kant and especially of Arthur Schopenhauer, who revered art, particularly classical music, above literally everything in life.

Art (but not music) also fascinated Heidegger. He particularly admired the ancient Greek Temple of Aphaia on the island of Aegina, one of the best preserved in the Greek world whose heroic simplicity appealed to many people at the time. Heidegger's admiration extended to a picture as simple as Van Gogh's painting of a pair of old shoes. Such works struck Heidegger as displaying *aletheia,* a Greek word he translated as unconcealment or disclosure. In an essay of 1936, *The Origins of the Work of Art*, Heidegger declared: 'The artist is the origin of the work. The work is the origin of the artist. Neither *is* without the other... To be a work means to set up a world... In setting up a world, the work sets forth the earth.' His insistence on the elemental and autonomous importance of a work of art had a great influence on his existentialist followers.

10 THINGS TO REMEMBER

1 *In the 1940s, Paris was a city uniquely welcoming to artists and thinkers.*

2 *Existentialists, unlike most philosophers, got on well with artistic radicals.*

3 *Merleau-Ponty detected in Cézanne's canvases a 'fruitful morbidity'.*

4 *Many artists in the 1940s, such as Dubuffet, thought of themselves as existentialists.*

5 *Sartre saw in the artist making original work from nothing a paradigm of authentic human existence.*

6 *Sartre regarded both Wols and Giacometti as artists of true* angoisse.

7 *Merleau-Ponty used painting to illustrate the human body's relation to the world.*

8 *Some philosophers (as far back as Plotinus) revered art as highly important.*

9 *Artists such Taslitzky and Picasso were Communists when most existentialists were not.*

10 *Heidegger thought works of art were as 'autonomous' as the artist creating them.*

8

Existentialism and religion

In this chapter you will learn:

- *that there are both theist and atheist approaches to existentialism*
- *how some theologians used existential ideas and language*
- *the implications of an existentialist view of 'God'*

Religion has always been existentialist. That may seem a curious statement to those who see existentialism as attempting to overthrow all traditional philosophy, and with it the metaphysics upon which religious beliefs have generally been based. But religion is not simply a matter of accepting certain beliefs. Religion is first and foremost a way of life, a commitment, a way of seeing and valuing. That way of life is expressed through beliefs, but it is generally true to say that for a religious person, those beliefs are not accepted in a detached or impersonal way, but are the basis of a personal engagement.

So religion focuses exactly on those things with which existentialism is concerned – commitment, choice and making sense of a life that is finite and ambiguous.

We find the origin of existential issues being discussed in the earliest religious traditions. Karl Jaspers describes as the 'axial age' a period from about 550 BCE when humankind started to move away from a mythological form of thinking to ask existential questions about the meaning and fragility of human life. From that age we have the Hebrew prophets, the earliest Greek thinkers, Confucius, Lao Tzu and the Buddha.

It is also widely recognized that, within the Christian tradition, Saint Augustine (354–430) explored the significance of Christianity in existential terms. He spoke of the depth of the self and its restless longings, of experiencing the self in terms of past, present and future, and exploring the place of religion in giving what one might now refer to as authenticity. The same could be said of many other religious figures. Luther, Kierkegaard and nineteenth-century revivalism all exemplified the religious demand for existential commitment.

So it is hardly surprising that, when it comes to twentieth-century existentialism, we find a range of attitudes towards religion.

The religious divide

Since Sartre, the key figure in twentieth-century existentialism, was an atheist, there is a tendency to assume that atheism is the existentialist norm. But this is neither logical nor true to the historical record. Many existentialist thinkers were religious, even if unconventionally so.

This is illustrated by those two great precursors of the existentialist movement, Kierkegaard and Nietzsche: the one profoundly religious, the other defiantly atheist. But that division continued within what we would think of as the mainstream of existentialist thinkers. Merleau-Ponty and Marcel were Catholic, Buber was Jewish, whereas Sartre, de Beauvoir and Camus were atheist.

But this simple division is not very helpful. Kierkegaard, seen as representing the religious tradition, fought against the conventional religious attitudes of his day, while Nietzsche, in his atheism, had an intensity and a commitment to human transcendence which has religious characteristics. Karl Jaspers was hardly a conventional religious believer, describing his position as one of having 'philosophical faith', and yet his views are profoundly religious, and he saw the striving of the secular philosopher as parallel to that of the believer.

In addition, there were a number of theologians who developed clearly existentialist ways of interpreting religious ideas. Bultmann, Tillich and Barth, major figures in twentieth-century theology, all used existential themes and language.

Probably the best way to understand how existentialism can come in both theistic and atheistic forms is to go back to the experience of radical contingency – the awareness that neither we nor anything else needs to exist; we are not our own explanation; we do not generate our own life; we might just as easily not exist at all.

From an atheist point of view, this fact of contingency is just a given feature of life. Because there is no external guarantor of meaning, we are challenged to give our own lives meaning by our choices and by affirming ourselves and striving for authenticity. But focus for a moment on that experience of contingency. I need not exist, but I *do exist*. My life does not provide its own explanation – it is just given to me, I have been 'thrown' (to use Heidegger's term) into this world. That can lead to a sense that the world is meaningless and absurd. But it can equally lead to the sense that the world is freely 'given', with a natural response in terms of gratitude, that, in spite of all the odds, I do actually exist. I have not created myself, but nevertheless I am here.

Lyrical existentialism

David Cooper in *Existentialism* (1990) calls Buber's *I and Thou* 'existentialism's most lyrical work'. Written in 1922, before existentialism had defined itself and blossomed as a separate philosophy, Buber's book explored the difference between the personal and impersonal ways of encountering the world.

In a wonderful opening – a model of clarity – Buber says that the world is twofold for man, reflecting a twofold attitude and two pairs of words: 'I-You' and 'I-It'. They establish two modes of existence. 'The world as experience belongs to the basic word I-It. The basic word I-You establishes the world of relation' (p. 56).

In other words, when I meet someone as a person, I address a 'You' and engage with them in a relationship. On the other hand, if I stand back from them, looking at them in a detached way, they become part of the world as experienced as 'I-It'. So here we find anticipated the fundamental division that we have already considered in terms of Sartre's 'in-itself' and 'for-itself'. 'I require a You to become; becoming I, I say You. All actual life is encounter' (p. 62, translation by Kaufman, T&T Clark, 1970).

He sees love as a quality within a relationship, rather than a set of experiences, and (in what is surely an anticipation of 'bad faith') he sees the possibility of the I-It world growing over a person 'like weeds'.

Buber also shows the difference between a person and an ego:

▶ *'Egos appear by setting themselves apart from other egos. Persons appear by entering into relation to other persons.'* (p. 112)
▶ *'The person says, "I am"; the ego says, "That is how I am." '*
▶ *'By setting himself apart from others, the ego moves away from being.'* (pp. 113–14)

(Contd)

Buber's main point is that experience can yield only an 'It', not a 'You' – for that requires personal engagement and encounter. His openness to the experience of the You introduces an existential approach to the idea of God. Not a god of the world of I-It, but an eternal 'You'.

Karl Jaspers introduced the idea of the 'encompassing' – an overall reality (prior to the split between objective and subjective) with which human beings could engage, and of which science was able to understand only that which is subsequently described as objective. This clearly has religious implications. For Jaspers, there is a philosophical quest for what he called Transcendence, a quest which is carried out using 'ciphers' – symbols which express transcendence – and which is religious but undogmatic. In his *Philosophical Faith and Revelation*, 1962, he says:

> **Preaching in church and conjuring Transcendence in philosophy refer to the same thing. The difference is that conjuration is a free, critical movement in ciphers, while a sermon is bound to proclaim the revelation.**

Philosophical Faith and Revelation, p. 357 (Collins, 1967)

> **For the controversy between theology and philosophy to disappear, the things proclaimed in church would have to shed their character of revealed realities, dogmas, and creeds – in other words, their proclamation would have to become a conjuration of ciphers.**

Philosophical Faith and Revelation, p. 357

Indeed, Jaspers passionately argues that this may indeed be the only way forward for religion, if it wants to engage with what he calls 'the hidden forces of truth in the modern masses.' But how might this work? To see this, we need to go back from this later reflection of Jaspers to the earlier work of Bultmann and Tillich.

Bultmann and Tillich

Heidegger moved to the University of Marburg in 1923, where he started writing *Being and Time*, finishing and publishing it in 1927. At Marburg he worked briefly alongside two theologians who were to display profoundly existential themes in their work: Rudolph Bultmann and Paul Tillich. The three were never close colleagues, and the only contact between Heidegger and Tillich was said to be through students who moved between their lectures, but Heidegger's work was still influential.

Bultmann, in his work on the New Testament, pointed out that the biblical narratives should not be taken in a literal sense, but as stories that were concerned to produce a response in their hearers (or later, their readers). Texts were written for a purpose and should be seen in the context in which they were originally used – they should not be mistaken for simple, factual accounts.

There is a huge and important issue at stake here, one that has profound implications for the nature of religion. If religious language is taken literally, a person stands in the wrong relationship to it. The world, and individual events within it, can be examined scientifically. We may analyse events to see how they are caused and so on. Some events may be inexplicable, for some we may have insufficient evidence to know whether the accounts we have of them are correct or not. But the issue of the truth or otherwise of any statements at that factual level is of intellectual interest only.

Factual statements and proofs do not challenge us at a personal level. For that to happen, you need to get behind the factual to engage with stories that speak of the meaning and purpose of life.

So how does this relate to the New Testament, or indeed to belief in God? At one level, it is possible simply to examine textual evidence for how the scriptures came to be written, or to examine and weigh up rational arguments for or against belief in God. But these things do not in themselves engage us as human beings. I may study and know every word in the New Testament without thereby becoming religious.

So Bultmann and others took the step that had already been explored in the nineteenth century by Kierkegaard. They pointed out that what mattered was the existential interpretation of narratives, not their factual content. The language of the scriptures is often mythological. Stories about going up into heaven are not intended to prove that there are limits to what gravity can do, but to express an existential commitment to the idea that this person is highly valued – literally, belonging in the heavenly realm. But of course, even the idea of a 'heavenly realm' is itself a myth, a way of expressing value, compared with the ambiguous values encountered on Earth.

Biblical scholarship therefore distinguished fact from myth, not to discredit its veracity, but to show how it should be used. The purpose of most stories that ended up in the New Testament was given in the context of worship or teaching. To appreciate their mythological nature is therefore to see what they were intended to 'say' to the reader or listener.

The implication of all this is that God is not to be treated as an object – something detached and external – but as a quality of personal experience, the eternal 'You' of Buber's work.

As thinkers like Heidegger were criticizing the dualism of Descartes – where the thinking self looked out on a separate, external world and questioned its existence – so Bultmann, Tillich and other theologians were to point to the folly of seeing religion as a matter of looking out towards (and attempting to believe in) an external, supernatural world. The purpose of religious stories was never to give information, but to explore personal values and commitments. Religion becomes a function of the human spirit – the 'transcending' (going beyond) of mundane life – not belief in a collection of pre-scientific theories.

The younger man, Paul Tillich – who was to produce his *Systematic Theology* in New York while Sartre was promoting existentialism in Paris – argued that God is characterized by two things:

▸ *God is 'Being-itself', not a particular being*
▸ *God is 'ultimate concern'*

Both concepts relate to the work of Heidegger, and both are key to an existentialist approach to religion. Tillich emphasized that the idea of God is related to the whole nature of our experience of Being – he cannot be simply one among other things that we encounter in the world. And just as Heidegger saw our involvement in the world as a matter of our 'concern', Tillich saw the word 'God' as indicating our ultimate concern, the commitment and challenge to deal with life as a whole.

The crucial thing to recognize with Tillich's thought is that what most people think of as 'God' – namely a being who might or might not exist 'out there' somewhere – is a modern form of idolatry. It is not just that such a God does not exist, which is the rather unnecessary argument put out by many atheists, but that the very idea of such a God deflects attention from the real object of religion, namely 'Being itself'.

Being itself is beyond existence and non-existence. So, in *Systematic Theology*, Tillich is able to say that 'God does not exist', because to say that he exists is to make him an object among objects, and that is idolatry. His own way of describing God is as 'the ground of our being', an idea taken up by John Robinson in *Honest to God*, the book that challenged conventional religious ideas in the 1960s.

Insight

It is difficult to overstate the significance of this shift within religious thought. Too often neglected since the days of radical theology in the 1960s and 70s, it provided an intellectual framework for ideas that may be traced back to Augustine Luther, Kierkegaard and many other religious thinkers. Its neglect leads to the often sad confrontation between fundamentalist believers and equally fundamentalist atheists – twin forms of modern idolatry.

We have already seen the way in which existential thought tries to balance 'facticity' and 'transcendence': in other words, we find ourselves thrown into a particular situation, but at the same time we go beyond, or 'transcend' it. Tillich argued that all religious knowledge came by way of symbols, and that a symbol (unlike a sign, which may be entirely conventional) makes real as well as pointing to that which it symbolizes. Thus, for example, a road sign is just that, a sign; we know what it means because we have been taught it. On the other hand, a luxury car or watch may be taken as a 'symbol' of wealth – not because we have been taught that the one points to the other, but simply because it expresses and makes real that wealth.

So, in Tillich's theology, the eternal is unknowable, except through the vehicle of concrete things that point beyond themselves. Just as the self vanishes if it is considered in an objective and analytic way, so religion vanishes if it does not appreciate this personal and self-transcending quality of experience.

The Courage to Be

In 1952 Tillich published *The Courage to Be,* a title which clearly echoes existentialist themes. The courage of which he spoke was 'the self-affirmation of being in spite of the fact of nonbeing' and he relates it directly to his description of God as 'being itself': 'Everything that is participates in being-itself, and everybody has some awareness of this participation, especially in the moments in which he experiences the threat of nonbeing...'

Tillich wants to get rid of the God of 'theological theism' – a being, rather than being itself:

God appears as the invincible tyrant, the being in contrast with whom all other beings are without freedom and subjectivity... He is equated with the recent tyrants who with the help of terror try to transform everything into a mere object, a thing among things, a cog in the machine they control. He becomes the model of everything against which existentialism revolted. This is the God Nietzsche said had to be killed because nobody can tolerate being made into a mere object of absolute knowledge and absolute control. This is the deepest root of atheism.

The Courage to Be, section 2, part b

The courage to take the anxiety and meaninglessness upon oneself is the boundary line up to which the courage to be can go. Beyond it is mere nonbeing. Within it all forms of courage are re-established in the power of the God above the God of theism. The courage to be is rooted in the God who appears when God has disappeared in the anxiety of doubt.

The Courage to Be, from the end of section 2

Protestant and Catholic

If Heidegger's thought influenced the radical wing of biblical
and systematic theology, it had an equal impact on the more
traditional Protestant approach. The idea of personal commitment
is absolutely central to the thinking of Karl Barth, a prominent
Protestant theologian. Following a tradition which predates
existentialism and has its roots in the Protestant Reformation
of the sixteenth century, this approach to theology is suspicious
of all metaphysics. The first thing is to be committed, that is the
basis of faith; understanding is very much secondary. This reflects
a tradition that sees human reason as essentially 'fallen' and
therefore unable to understand God. The divine is reached only
by faith – by a leap (to use Kierkegaard's term).

Insight

The danger of this approach is that it slips into a
fundamentalism that can only proclaim itself, not explain
itself. You are expected to set reason aside and make a
leap into a faith community. The problem with this is that
such a leap is totally at the mercy of the person or scripture
presenting the challenge and inviting the leap. It is then
difficult to get an objective assessment of beliefs, because
they are essentially taken on trust – one does not justify faith,
one simply expounds on it.

Among the prominent Catholic theologians who were influenced by
existentialism, Karl Rahner (1904–84) studied under Heidegger for
two years in the 1930s. He hoped to integrate some of his existential
insights into traditional Catholic thinking. He was convinced of the
need to locate the experience of God within the world. Being too
radical for some Catholic thinkers at the time, his thesis was rejected,
but was published in 1939 as *Geist im Welt* (*Spirit in the World*).

His thinking was focused on the question of man's quest for
meaning, reflecting the phenomenological ontology of Heidegger,
but considering it in the light of traditional religious concepts

such as grace. Like the existentialists, Rahner wanted to explore the human experience of being in the world, but at the same time saw man as straining to transcend the world. He sees God as the horizon of our experience of the world.

He was influenced by the whole tradition of Catholic thought that developed out of the work of the thirteenth century philosopher Thomas Aquinas, and also by his study of Kant, but it is worth noting that elements of the existentialist's embedding of human life in the experience of the world, rather than in metaphysical speculation about what lies beyond it, could find its place within his overall approach to Catholic thought. In particular, he saw philosophy as raising the question about human existence, to which theology can then explore possible answers.

This is hardly existentialist philosophy as we would recognize it in Sartre – not surprising, given Sartre's atheism and Rahner's Catholicism – but it shows a common starting point and movement from the experience of being here in the world towards a 'nothingness' (as in Sartre) or a transcendence that is, for Rahner, a God who is infinite reality and a mystery beyond human apprehension.

Spanish existentialists: Unamuno and Ortega y Gassett

The two great Spanish philosophers of the twentieth century, Miguel de Unamuno (1864–1936) and José Ortega y Gassett (1883–1955), are both seen as proto-existentialist. Unamuno, who was a romantic poet, playwright and novelist as well as a philosopher, rejected scientific scepticism, indeed reason, in his passionate quest for a meaning to life and death. In his most famous work, *The Tragic Sense of Life* (*Del Sentimiento Trágico de la Vida*, 1914), he argued for an attitude that will invest human life with a tragic but transcendent dignity, in spite of the huge

(Contd)

uncertainties facing us. 'Faith which does not doubt is not good faith', he declared (*The Agony of Christianity*). His heroes were Christ and Don Quixote, men who in their very different ways fulfilled their own missions. Unamuno's religious intensity recalls Pascal and especially Kierkegaard, whose 'leap of faith' he admired, but in his overall despair he is closer to Dostoyevsky. (Such a non-Catholic reading of Christianity led to Unamuno's books being put on the Index of Prohibited Books until 1962.)

In contrast to the tortured Unamuno, Ortega y Gassett was lucid, urbane and cosmopolitan, alert to the latest ideas from across Europe. He wrote on history, politics and aesthetics as well as metaphysics, epistemology and ethics. In his most famous work *The Revolt of the Masses* (*La Rebelión de las Masas*, 1930) he depicted modern societies as dominated by the masses and 'the commonplace mind'. His aristocratic liberalism led him to oppose dictatorships of the left or right and he quit Spain in 1936 to avoid Franco's regime. Ortega rejected Descartes' '*Cogito ergo sum*' as a sufficient explanation of reality. Instead he wrote: '*Yo soy yo y mi circunstancia*' ('I am myself and my circumstances'). A thing is real only in so far is it is rooted in, and figures in, my life. The self is not separated from its surroundings. A dynamic interaction with the external world shapes our own world, making every human life a drama played out between necessity and freedom. Ortega influenced Heidegger's masterwork *Being and Time*, the Old Testament of existentialism, and the thought of Hannah Arendt, Heidegger's most famous student.

Shifting the idea of 'God'

Remember the basic structures by which Heidegger analysed Dasein – that we exist as a self-in-the-world, and that the world, for us, is a framework of meaning and significance. We engage with it all the time, our experience coloured by our mood.

Now think back to the very opposite of all this – to Descartes or the empiricists. They held that there was a fundamental division between mind and matter. Mind was 'in here' doing the thinking, while the world was 'out there' to be examined by science. All that we could know of the world was transmitted to us via our senses, and we had to judge the extent to which we could be certain about the information they gave.

So when we make the shift to Heidegger's ontology and its existentialist implications, we find that it sets a whole new agenda in terms of religious belief. On the old, dualist way of thinking, there could be a debate about whether or not God existed – in other words, whether there was something external to ourselves that corresponded to the word 'God'. And the philosophy of religion has a long history of examining arguments about that.

But look what happens once you adopt the existentialist perspective. God is no longer thought of as 'a being' alongside others, but 'being itself'. God becomes the ultimate point of reference in that web, or network of meaning that I call 'world' and within which I am embedded.

For Heidegger, like Nietzsche, this is the only world there is, but that does not entirely eliminate language about God and religion. Thinkers like Schleiermacher (with his 'sense and taste for the infinite') and Otto (looking at the mysterious within religious experience), had already explored the nature of religious experience as something that is fully *within* this world.

Even though, as we have seen, many existentialists were confirmed atheists, religion, in the broad sense of that word, can make sense from an existential perspective since it offers values and commitments which may help people to 'transcend' their narrow self-interest. 'God', in such an existential approach to religion, becomes a term for the ultimate framework of meaning and value within which we find ourselves.

This follows what mystics and others have always affirmed, namely that God is not external to us but that we are at one with him. God certainly does not exist – because an existing thing (in the sense of something within the world that might be detectable by science) is certainly not what 'God' is about. God makes sense only within a self-world framework of meaning; a god who exists cannot be God.

The existentialist Buddha

The opening of the earliest collection of the Buddha's sayings, the *Dhammapada*, sets out his basic view that our life is the creation of our mind:

What we are today comes from our thoughts of yesterday
And our present thoughts build our life of tomorrow
Our life is the creation of our mind.

This process – of life being shaped by mind – does not imply a separate independent thinking self, of the Cartesian sort. Indeed, this is contrary to Buddhist thought, for it is a central feature of Buddhism that there is no fixed self. Rather, life is shaped by the process of thinking and choosing, and one has to take responsibility for that, since one lives with its results: karma. This is exactly the sort of personal challenge that existentialism also presents. It moves away from fixed beliefs, such as 'God' or a fixed, eternal soul, and instead sees the task of spiritual development and overcoming suffering as a mundane one of mindful awareness of each present moment and ethical response to it.

Existentialism in a nutshell!

The quest to be God

The division within existentialism between the religious and the atheists is really quite fundamental. Consider this:

If you believe that meaning and value are not to be found within the world that you experience and within which you are embedded, you may see it as your responsibility to construct your own values, to live forwards towards the future that you choose for yourself and your world. That is a basically atheist position, and it reflects the central appeal of the work of Sartre.

On the other hand, if you believe that life offers us opportunities to *discover* meaning and value in the world, rather than simply *impose* them on it, you may (or you may not) want to express that sense of 'Being Itself' in terms of 'God'. Like the atheist, you may take your commitments seriously, you may recognize your responsibility to shape the future, but it is all done in the context of a relationship with the sense you have of a source of meaning outside yourself.

So when it comes to issues of responsibility, commitment, self-transcendence, self-affirmation, the awareness of Angst and of death, both religious and atheist thinkers share a common set of existential features. When it comes to the source of values and of meaning, they diverge. For the atheist existentialist, God is banished along with all other traditional structures and ideas. For the religious existentialist, God is discovered at the point at which intellectual quests are set aside and one accepts commitment to what which cannot be proved.

Sartre, too, has a place for God within his philosophy – but predictably, it is related directly to the human project. He sees the for-itself as having a project to become 'the foundation of its own being-in-itself' and he then says:

> *It is this ideal which can be called God. Thus the best way to conceive of the fundamental project of human reality is to say that man is the being whose project is to be God. Whatever*

may be the myths and rites of the religion considered, God is first 'sensible to the heart' of man as the one who identifies and defines him in his ultimate and fundamental project ... God, value and supreme end of transcendence, represents the permanent limit in terms of which man makes known to himself what he is. To be man means to reach toward being God. Or if you prefer, man fundamentally is the desire to be God.

Being and Nothingness, p. 587

One of the most frequently quoted sentences from Sartre's *Being and Nothingness* is 'Man is a useless passion', but it is seldom set in context. It comes at the very end of part IV, just before he launches into his Conclusion, and it is worth considering the three sentences that precede it (p. 636):

Every human reality is a passion in that it projects losing itself so as to found being and by the same stroke to constitute the In-itself which escapes contingency by being its own foundation, the Enscausa sui, which religions call God. Thus the passion of man is the reverse of that of Christ, for man loses himself as man in order that God may be born. But the idea of God is contradictory and we lose ourselves in vain. Man is a useless passion.

In other words, the passion of Man is to establish value and meaning in something that is permanent, beyond the transient reality of all physical things in this world. That is the passion for God, a self-generating in-itself. But, of course, Sartre sees the attempt to lose the for-itself in order to absorb or be absorbed into the in-itself as something which involves Man losing himself. In other words, for Sartre, the passion for God achieves nothing but the loss of self. Man is always trying to establish himself, to be his own cause, to turn his consciousness into an in-itself – a defined, known essence – and man is always failing in that task.

Insight

The in-itself world of things is mindless, utterly different from the personal for-itself. But the idea of God is the attempt to give the in-itself a mind and personality. That is the fundamental problem with religion from the standpoint of atheistic existentialism.

Believers may argue that, without the idea of God, or of some established foundation, morality loses its base – anything is possible in a world without God. This argument is always going to be a challenge for the thoughtful atheist because, if the world does not provide any foundation for normative judgements, there is no definitive way of adjudicating between conflicting ideas of right or wrong, or of establishing values.

But the deeper issue is whether there is any scope, within a philosophy of self-generated meaning and value, for a sense that, in their self-world relationship, people may discover rather than create.

Insight

There is an old joke that General Charles de Gaulle, who came from the village of Colombey-les-Deux-Églises, was once asked why 'Deux Églises' and replied 'L'autre, c'est pour le Dieu!' His philosophical contemporary had a similar problem with God, for Sartre's atheism is not a denial of the sense of transcendence, but a transcendence located at the heart of human consciousness. With the human self firmly in creative control, shaping and giving meaning to its world, there is no room for another God.

But perhaps the final word on existentialism and religion should come from Karl Jaspers. Towards the end of *Philosophical Faith and Revelation*, looking for a 'practical seriousness' that might save the world from its present peril (perceived differently, no doubt, in 1962, but relevant still), he makes a comment that is utterly relevant to our assessment of existentialism:

Today, outside the churches, this seriousness is found only in the personal freedom of the individual. However potent for him, it is doomed to ineffectiveness in the great community of all. Its appearance in the world goes with the wind; philosophical faith does not yet emerge as a visible, strong, public phenomenon. It stays hidden away, thus far, in personal communication.

And the remedy, if the world is not to plunge into 'scientific superstition'...

Philosophy should do its level best to bring reason into the religious thinking of the churches, so that it may become believable for the informed masses – so every individual may find his human self in accord with that thinking, and may draw on it for the impulses to his decisions and his way of life. (p. 358)

It is important to grasp the significance of what is being argued for here:

▶ *Science deals with the objective aspect of reality – it becomes superstition if this is taken for the whole of human reality.*
▶ *Existential philosophy, although releasing the power of human* Existenz *in freedom and authentic living, is too focused on the individual.*
▶ *Religion is unbelievable unless it sheds its dogmatism and sees its task as exploring the ciphers (or symbols) of Transcendence.*

Insight

The implication of this, it seems to me, is that the existentialist way of understanding and engaging with the world needs to escape from a narrow individualism and recognize that its role is one that parallels religion, showing that human life thrives on the responsibility of its freedom and in the seriousness with which it creates and lives by its values. Religion could do this, had it not become unbelievable for many by holding to literal dogma when it should be freely exploring the symbols of transcendence.

10 THINGS TO REMEMBER

1 *Religion has always explored existential questions.*

2 *Twentieth-century existentialism includes both atheist and religious thinkers.*

3 *Buber distinguished 'I-It' and 'I-You' as modes of existence.*

4 *Jaspers sees parallels between religion and secular existentialist philosophy.*

5 *Bultmann and Tillich applied existential thinking to Christian theology.*

6 *Tillich sees God as 'being-itself' rather than a being.*

7 *Existentialism influenced both Barth (Protestant) and Rahner (Catholic).*

8 *In existentialist theology, God is the ultimate frame of reference.*

9 *Basic Buddhist teaching is existentialist.*

10 *Sartre saw man's 'useless passion' as wanting to be God.*

9

Authenticity and the absurd: the fiction of Sartre and Camus

In this chapter you will learn:
- *that fiction and drama can reveal existentialist ideas intellectually*
- *that Sartre and Camus explored the Absurd and authenticity in their fiction*
- *that the theatre of the Absurd anticipated or complemented existentialist ideas*

At any street corner the feeling of absurdity can strike a person in the face.

Camus, *The Myth of Sisyphus*

Several existentialists were novelists and playwrights as well as philosophers and two were outstanding. Both are still read around the world and both were offered the Nobel Prize for Literature (there is no prize for philosophy): Albert Camus, who humbly accepted the prize in 1957, and Jean-Paul Sartre, who proudly refused it in 1964 lest it jeopardize his independence. For the general reader, the fiction of both is often the most illuminating way to approach their philosophy. There is of course one notable difference between Sartre and Camus: the former was a great systematic philosopher who wrote major books of pure philosophy, most notably *Being and Nothingness* (1943); the latter only produced two short philosophical works, *The Myth of Sisyphus* (1942) and *The Rebel* (1951). However, both were superb novelists, exploring in fiction crucial themes of authenticity, freedom, responsibility, bad faith and the **Absurd**.

There are occasions when only literature can fully convey the subtle intricacies and dilemmas of the human condition. For Sartre and Camus, fiction at times clearly offered the best way to deal with the realities of the human condition *intellectually*. Sartre's first great novel *Nausea* (*La Nausée*, published 1938) gives a terrifying if marvellous sense of the contingency and absurdity of human life. There is no need for any technical philosophical language to appreciate the poetic heights – or tragic depths – of it or his other novels, *The Roads to Freedom* trilogy, or of Camus' *The Outsider* and *The Plague*. Sartre's plays such as *Huis Clos* (*No Exit*) have also entered the repertory. This chapter investigates existentialism as it is expounded through the fiction of Sartre and Camus.

Philosophers and fiction

Sartre and Camus were not the only philosophers to write great literature. Plato's dialogues (fourth century BCE) can approach the state of fiction, so brilliantly do they portray character and emotion; Lucretius wrote his defence of Epicurean philosophy *De rerum natura* (*c.* 60 BCE) as a superb lyric poem; Voltaire wrote *Candide* (1759) as a dazzling satirical novel partly to attack Leibniz's over-optimistic philosophy; de Beauvoir wrote novels that are still admired; and Iris Murdoch is now much better known as a novelist than as a philosopher.

THE WALL

Sartre wrote many short stories from an early age. One was recognized as a masterpiece from the moment of its publication in *La Nouvelle Revue Française* in 1937, *The Wall* ('*Le Mur*'). It was hailed by the critic Gaëtan Picon as 'pure, naked and full'. Set during the Spanish Civil War (1936–9), *The Wall* focuses on the psychology of three prisoners condemned to death without trial and awaiting execution at dawn. Through them, Sartre explores differing reactions to the knowledge of imminent death. (We all know that we will die, of course, but dismiss it as an unthinkably distant event.) The wall of the title is the wall against which the three men will be lined up and shot, into which the bullets will lodge after smashing through their bodies, the wall which they wish they could 'get inside' to escape the volleys. It also symbolizes the fixed limit set to every life.

Pablo Ibbieta is the narrator, an unheroic one despite his determination to 'die cleanly.' He looks without sympathy at Juan, the youngest of the prisoners sobbing pathetically. When Juan asks the doctor watching them, 'Does it [being shot] hurt much?' he gets an evasive reply. Ibbieta himself is sweating with a fear he does not like to acknowledge, while Tom the third prisoner wets his pants in terror. Ibbieta's mood in the cell is deeply nihilistic as he looks back on a life which 'was worth nothing because it was finished. I wondered how I had been able to walk, to laugh with girls; I wouldn't have moved as much as my little finger if I had ever imagined I would die like this.'

Insight

Ibbieta finds the Fascist officers interrogating him absurd, not intimidating. 'These men all dolled up with their riding crops and boots were still going to die. A little later than me, but not much… Their petty activities seemed shocking and burlesque to me… I couldn't put myself in their place.' Here Sartre stresses the existential truth that, seen in the light of eternity (*sub specie aeternatis*, as Spinoza put it), all our actions are essentially futile. Exactly when people are busying themselves with causes they think important enough to justifying killing others, they are at their most absurd.

Offered his life by the Fascists in exchange for information about Gris, another wanted Republican, Ibbieta at first refuses. Then, to annoy his captors and buy time, he gives what he thinks is false information: Gris is hiding in the cemetery. Finding himself to his amazement reprieved, he hears from a man newly arrested that Gris has been found and shot. Gris had moved from his original hiding place – to the cemetery. 'I laughed so much I cried', Ibbieta says, and the story ends abruptly, discordantly.

Insight

Heidegger called death one's 'ownmost' thing. Everything else you might do in life could be done by someone else, but dying is something you have to do yourself. Unlike Heidegger, who therefore sees us all as beings-towards-death, Sartre does not think people experience their lives as progressing towards death. Someone who sees his death closer today than yesterday, as if using up a fixed quota, is mistaken, for his date of death is not predetermined. Only someone condemned to death has such a quota, but even he may be reprieved.

The reasonable, the absurd and the responsible...

For Camus 'the absurd' is the result of the radical mismatch between our expectations that the world will have a meaning and purpose, and our actual experience of life as meaningless, random and impersonal. Accepting and challenging the absurd nature of the world makes for authentic existence. But to say that something is absurd suggests that it *might have been* rational and explicable. The fall of dice cannot be called absurd for there is no logic to predict how dice will fall. Things are only 'absurd' if we assume that they *should* follow a particular pattern but do not.

So the absurd view of life is not wholly exclusive to existentialism. Any view that accepts that events are random, not following patterns that are humanly explicable, will accept that life fails to meet our expectations and so may be called 'absurd'. However, existentialism positively rejoices in the absurdity of life because absurdity thrusts people back onto themselves and their own choices. If the events that shape life come totally at random, not determined by something or someone else (History or God), then we have no choice but to accept responsibility for our own actions and live with the consequences.

Sartre wrote *Nausea* (published in 1938) over six years, mostly while working as a philosophy teacher in Le Havre, a job he disliked but to which he returned after studying in Germany. The port is the model for Bouville, the novel's dismal setting. *Nausea* had great immediate success, enabling its author to move permanently back to Paris. It can be read at two levels: as an expression in fictional form of Sartre's metaphysical thought, anticipating theories developed in *Being and Nothingness*; or, in a literary sense, as an exploration of the problems of writing about a character writing a journal about doing nothing.

Insight

Nausea seamlessly fuses fiction and philosophy. Iris Murdoch, Sartre's profoundest critic in English, considered it 'more like a poem or incantation than a novel' but also saw it as his 'most densely philosophical novel'.

The novel is written as the journal of Antoine Roquentin, a gloomily introspective 30-year-old recluse who could be Sartre's alter ego. Returning to Bouville after years away, Roquentin is supposedly doing research for his biography of the Marquis de Robellon, an obscure eighteenth-century figure whose papers are in the local museum. In practice he simply wanders around the town thinking about the lack of meaning or purpose in his life.

Living almost completely alone, he experiences time as an endless caravan of dreary days passing. 'Nothing happens while you live. The scenery changes, people come in and go out, that's all... Days are tacked onto days without rhyme or reason, an interminable, monotonous addition.' Roquentin lives in a cheap hotel room, has almost no possessions and attempts only the most desultory writing. Even his memories of the past are jejune. 'However much I trawl through the past, I can only recover scraps of images and I don't know what they represent, nor if they are remembered or invented.'

Knowing that the future does not really exist – a knowledge most of us deny under the delusion that the future will somehow make us 'complete' – fills Roquentin with nausea. Nausea is the horrifying sense of the total contingency and absurdity of our existence. It attacks him like a vicious migraine and pervades everything. 'Nausea is not inside me: I feel it out there in the wall … everywhere around me. It makes itself one with the café, I am the one who is *within it*.'

One of his nausea attacks is triggered by seeing in Bouville Museum portraits of dead burghers that depict them as taller and nobler – less **contingent** – than the Victorian haut bourgeois ever actually were. Typical of the type Roquentin hates is the 'handsome, impeccable' Jean Pacôme, whose 'magnificent grey eyes had never been clouded by the smallest doubt. Nor had Pacôme ever made a mistake.' Another bout of nausea is caused by an inoffensive old chestnut tree in a park. Its softness, stickiness and corpulence strike Roquentin as disgustingly, excessively *en soi* (in-itself, like all objects) and flabbily feminine in its 'soft, monstrous masses in disorder – naked, with a frightening, obscene nakedness'. (There is a misogynistic streak in Roquentin stemming perhaps from his author.)

Ultimately his nausea stems from grasping the mysteriously *contingent* existence of the universe as a whole, a realization that most human activities are implicitly designed to avoid. Roquentin in fact has had a quasi-mystical vision, albeit one of despair.

Insight

The concept of contingency is central to *Nausea* and to Sartre's philosophical vision. What is *contingent* is not logically necessary. It does not have to exist and natural processes will cause it to end, unlike that which is *necessary*, which is beyond nature and so unaffected by natural processes. For more on radical contingency see the section on Nothingness above (p. 59–61).

There is one other significant character in Bouville, Ogier P, whom Roquentin calls the Autodidact. A passionate socialist and humanist, he is trying to acquire all human knowledge available in the local library, learning facts by heart in alphabetical order. Devoid of personal charm and friends, he tries to befriend Roquentin but only provokes a new attack of nausea in him. Towards the novel's end, the Autodidact is caught stroking a schoolboy's hand in the library. Punched in the face, he is thrown out by the attendant and barred from the library, so ruining his life. Roquentin feels a sudden flash of pity for the Autodidact but his belated offer of help is refused.

Although a recluse, Roquentin has, or had, a girlfriend, Anny. She lives in Paris and dreams of their having 'perfect moments' together that they somehow never achieve. The thought of seeing her again after long separation fills him with unusual excitement and their reunion is described with touching honesty, free of sentimentality. Although Anny is now older and fatter, he finds himself falling in love again, but she declares that she has 'outlived herself' and developed an attitude to life that mirrors his. Unable to offer her any hope or reason for living, they part for good although still half in love. Back in Bouville, Roquentin realizes he is now utterly alone. Refusing to yield to what would be (for him) the luxury of total despair, Roquentin decides to leave Bouvillle and write a novel. Doing so will both justify his existence and distract him from it.

Nausea remains an astonishing novel. Though rooted in the French realist tradition, it bears comparison with Dostoyevsky's almost pathologically intense works such as *Notes from Underground* and *Crime and Punishment*. William Barrett wrote in *Irrational Man: A Study in Existential Philosophy* that *Nausea* 'may well be Sartre's best book for the very reason that in it the intellectual and the creative artist come closest to being conjoined.' If Sartre had written nothing else, he would still be remembered as a great author.

Why does Sartre always have to be so gloomy?

Simone de Beauvoir's young sister Hélène typed up the manuscripts of *The Age of Reason* that Sartre sent her during the winter of 1939–40 while serving as a soldier. Writing to Simone, she said: 'Typing Sartre's works always fills me with gloom but talking to him is wonderful… Living up to one's neck in his work is awful. I hope that inside himself he is not like the characters he portrays in his books, for then his life would be almost intolerable.' Many readers have since felt the same. For such a widely read writer, Sartre is remarkably depressing. (His original title for *Nausea* was *Melancholia*.) The sparse humour to be found in his books is ironic and dry. One or two critics have even accused Sartre of laughing at his readers under his sleeve, but this would be such an act of bad faith on his part that the charge can be dismissed.

Very different factors explain his apparent pessimism. The books of other perennially popular writers – Dostoyevsky and Kafka, for example – do not provide many laughs. Nor does every writer want to entertain his audience as Charles Dickens did. Sartre was dealing, in his novels and plays as in his formal philosophy, with the weightiest subjects imaginable: death, war, guilt. These are bound to disturb and at first to depress readers. He himself wrote: 'It seems to me that the ensemble of my books will be optimistic, because through that ensemble the whole will be reconstituted, although each of my characters is a cripple.' Sartre may often show humans at their worst – small-minded, cowardly, selfish – but he also offers a possibility of freedom that will transform human life positively. He stands in the high tradition of philosophical moralists going back to Socrates, who strip us of comforting delusions to make us free.

After *Nausea* Sartre started what became a trilogy of novels: *The Roads to Freedom* (*Les chemins de la liberté*). At the same time he was writing *Being and Nothingness*, the twin tasks occupying him through the grimmest days of the Second World War. As he worked, he gradually changed from a thinker mainly concerned with the personal to one fully aware of the political. The three books, exploring in fictional form philosophical concepts of freedom, commitment and responsibility, reflect this change.

The first novel, *The Age of Reason* (*L'âge de raison,* published 1945), is set in Paris over two days in June 1938. Its hero Mathieu Delarue, a young philosophy teacher like Sartre, lives a bohemian life loafing around cafés, avoiding commitments. Vaguely supporting the Republican cause in the Spanish Civil War, he refuses to get involved despite warnings from Brunet, a Communist sympathetically portrayed, that they will all soon be at war. Mathieu's chief concern is finding the money to pay for an abortion for his girlfriend Marcelle. Her pregnancy threatens his independence.

Insight

Sartre's own distaste for children comes over clearly here. He considered having children almost a cop-out, a way for people to live vicariously while abandoning their true duty to be free.

Mathieu is forced to ask for help from his rich brother Jacques, a Nazi-sympathizing bourgeois *salaud* (bastard) who wants him to marry Marcelle. Daniel Sereno, a closet homosexual, also tries to persuade Mathieu to marry Marcelle before proposing to her himself. By denying his sexuality, Daniel is acting in bad faith – an existentialist sin. (Sartre had no objection to homosexuality per se.) Finally Daniel confesses his homosexuality to Mathieu, who is not 'greatly astonished' but wonders at Daniel's seeming willingness for such marital martyrdom.

The next novel *The Reprieve* (*Le sursis*, published 1945), is set in September 1938 during the Munich crisis, with France and Britain seemingly about to go to war with Germany over Czechoslovakia. Earlier characters reappear along with many new ones: workers, peasants, soldiers, prostitutes. Two salient factors shape the book: Mathieu, about to be called up into the army, determines to welcome his fate and the possibility of death, not for patriotic but for individualistic reasons; and Daniel, bored by marriage to Marcelle, has a bogus religious experience in which he becomes convinced that God is looking after him: 'I am seen, therefore I am,' he writes in a letter to Mathieu. 'I need no longer bear the responsibility of my turbid, disintegrating self.' Daniel has fallen into bad faith, existentialism's cardinal sin, regarding himself as an unfree homosexual thing (en soi) rather than a self-determining man (pour soi).

The third novel, *Iron in the Soul* (*La mort dans l'âme*, published 1949), opens in June 1940 as France falls to the Nazis. The collapse threatens everyone's lives and their varying reactions – their courage or cowardice – dominate the book. Daniel rejoices in the fall of a world that despised him, becoming a sexual predator; Jacques joins the panicking exodus of Parisians fleeing the city, quarrelling en route with his wife over why he has done so – both inauthentic reactions. Mathieu, caught up in the rout, joins some soldiers still fighting the Germans and dies in a doomed last stand. In doing so he achieves final authenticity. 'He fired. He was cleansed. He was all-powerful. He was free.' The last part of the book focuses on the Communist Brunet. Captured as a prisoner of war, he bravely accepts his being-in-situation (as Sartre did), overcoming near-starvation by disciplined willpower. Brunet sees most of the prisoners as weakly self-indulgent, longing only for leadership. With Schneider, a fellow prisoner, Brunet talks at length about the Soviet Union and its relations with French Communism – something Sartre himself would later do.

All three novels were well received but can today seem didactic compared to *Nausea*. In 1945 Sartre began what would have been the final novel of a tetralogy, *The Last Chance* (*La dernière chance*), but he never finished it. In plays, however, he found another way of expounding his thinking in accessible form. Two he wrote in the 1940s are among his finest.

THE FLIES

Sartre wrote and staged his first play, *Bariona*, as a prisoner of war in December 1940. Its anti-Nazi message eluded his German captors, who failed to realize it was not really a nativity play. Back in Paris in 1941, he began writing *The Flies* (*Les Mouches*). Premiered in June 1943, it is set in ancient Greece, which helped it pass the censor. (The plot echoes that of the Greek tragedy *Libation Bearers* by Aeschylus, but with no god as final saviour.)

Orestes, a prince calling himself Philebus, returns to his native Argos. His father King Agamemnon was murdered there 14 years earlier by Aegistheus, who has seized the throne and married Orestes' mother Clytemnestra. Argos swarms with flies, symbols of moral corruption. Zeus, the god, urges Orestes to leave Argos and continue on his way – Zeus is enjoying the citizens' feelings of guilt. Orestes meets his sister Electra and his mother, neither of whom recognizes him, and offers to help Electra escape. She refuses, feeling she has to avenge her father. Orestes now realizes *he* must be the avenger and rid Argos of its fly-ridden remorse. He kills Aegistheus and Clytemnestra, accepting full responsibility but rejecting any guilt. 'I have performed my deed, Electra, and it was a good deed,' he declares, but Electra, guilt-ridden, begs Zeus for forgiveness for her part in the murders. Refusing the throne, Orestes quits Argos, taking the flies with him.

The Flies examines central existentialist themes of responsibility and freedom. Orestes, though unprepared for having to kill his mother, resists the temptation to say 'I was not meant for this' and walk away. Instead, he wins authenticity by rising to the challenge, proclaiming his will against Zeus – a symbol of corrupt authority as much as a god – so demonstrating the limitless power of human freedom. Electra, in contrast, relapses into bad faith when she prays for absolution from Zeus. The play was a rallying cry to occupied France at the time and to many oppressed peoples since. Its message is clear: violence must be fought with violence, there is no easy way out for cowards.

Cowardice, an existentialist sin

If authenticity is the greatest virtue for existentialists, cowardice ranks among the worst failings. Sartre personally knew what cowardice and courage meant. He had served in the army (if, like most French soldiers in 1940, without doing any fighting), had been a prisoner of war and then supported the Resistance in Paris, if with his pen rather than guns. Later he faced down threats from the Communist left as well as the right, for his writing enraged many. So he needed physical courage. Even more vital was moral courage to face the realities of existence. All around him he saw people, frightened of being free, deny their own predicaments and seek refuge in endless lame excuses.

NO EXIT

Sartre's next play *No Exit* (*Huis Clos*, also called *In Camera* or *Behind Closed Doors*) opened in May 1944 at the Théâtre du Vieux-Colombier in Paris. It was a great success, its message resonating in a city still under German occupation. It contains Sartre's most famous line, 'Hell is other people' (*L'enfer c'est les autres*). This is not as misanthropic as it sounds when seen in context, for the context is hell.

The play opens with a servant ushering Joseph Garcin into a claustrophobic over-furnished room without windows or mirrors. It becomes clear that Garcin is dead and in hell. Surprised to see no instruments of torture, he is informed by the servant that sleep – even closing one's eyes – is impossible and there is no way out, no relief or distraction from the relentless pressure of eternal reality. A hellish prospect, but reality involves other people and into the room are ushered in sequence two women: Inès Serrano, a lesbian postal clerk and Estelle Rigault, a vacuous society blonde. After their entry, the door is closed and locked. None has had any earlier connection with the others but all are now condemned to their mutual company for eternity. They are also doomed to torture each other mentally. (Each represents a significantly different stratum of the bourgeoisie: Garcin is a bourgeois intellectual, Inès a petty bourgeois clerk, Estelle a rich bourgeois.)

All, as they question one other, finally reveal why they are there: Garcin is a coward, an army deserter, cruelly unfaithful to his wife; Inès has driven another woman to suicide by manipulating and taunting her; Estelle has drowned a baby she had by her lower-class lover. Each is desperate to win over one of the others: Garcin wants the good opinion of Inès, who is trying to seduce Estelle, who is trying to seduce Garcin... Their bickerings intensify until Garcin suddenly demands an exit. 'Open the door! Open, damn you! I'll suffer anything, red-hot tongs, molten lead… anything is better than this mental agony.' But when the door suddenly flies open, he refuses to move. So does Inès. She too is a coward, he discovers.

The point of this blackest of comedies is not to depict an afterlife that makes oblivion seem enticing but to examine a key aspect of our life on earth: the existence of other people and the crippling effect this can have on us when we are 'being-for-others'. Subject to the judgement and freedom of the Other, we are at their mercy, 'enslaved' in Sartre's words. In short, hell is indeed other people – at least in such an infernal room without windows, books, sleep, darkness, work, tears, nature or any other escape.

Sartre continued to write plays such as *The Respectful Prostitute* (*La putain respectueuse*, 1946) and *Dirty Hands* (*Les mains sales*, 1948) but his real interests were increasingly political, not literary, as these plays attest.

Sartre, a bourgeois anti-bourgeois

Sartre was born into the ranks of the most respectable upper bourgeoisie. (A cousin on his mother's side was Albert Schweitzer, the revered theologian, philosopher and physician who won the Nobel Peace Prize in 1952.) An unhealthy child, he grew up in comfortable claustrophobia before going to the best schools and universities. He then became a teacher, a petty bourgeois profession. Yet he spent his life attacking the bourgeois, often depicting them as *salauds* (bastards/swine) if not as outright Nazi sympathizers like Jacques Delarue in *The Roads to Liberty*. This sort of attack, long predating his conversion to Marxist fellow-traveller, was common in the mid-twentieth century when Communist proletarian utopia seemed our inescapable future, not a discredited cliché. For Sartre however, given his upbringing, such attacks were probably a deep-rooted psychological necessity. But Sartre never cared to look into his unconscious.

Camus' novels

Camus' fiction rivals Sartre's in its intellectual power and, for many readers, surpasses it in literary appeal. In a way his work stands at an opposite pole to Sartre's. Its final note is not one of Sartrean disgust and nausea at existence but of rejoicing in physical reality despite everything. Camus' novels, like his plays and essays, wrestle with a central dilemma: Is life worth living in a universe that strips us of all significance, or is suicide the honest solution? He reached a positive but tough-minded conclusion: Yes, life is worth the struggle but only if we are prepared to face both its absurdity and our own consequent futility. Conor Cruise O'Brien, an often unsympathetic critic, conceded that 'to a generation which saw no reason for hope, it [Camus' work] offered hope without reason... it allowed the joy of being alive in the presence of death to emerge.'

Typical of Camus' 'Yes-saying' – *Ja sagen*, to borrow one of Nietzsche's favourite phrases – is the ending of his novel *The Outsider* (*L'Etranger*, also called *The Stranger*, published 1942). The hero or narrator Meursault, sentenced to death for a murder he has committed almost absent-mindedly and for which he feels no remorse, greets his last day on earth lyrically: 'Gazing up at the dark sky spangled with its signs and stars for the first time, I laid my heart open to the benign indifference of the universe. To feel it so like myself, indeed so brotherly, made me realize that I'd been happy and was happy still.'

Camus could view life on the shores of his native Mediterranean ecstatically and was wonderful at evoking the physical joys of such a life. 'What does eternity matter to me? To lose the touch of flowers and women's hands is the supreme separation,' he wrote in an essay on the Roman ruins of Djemila in Algeria. But he did not suggest a happy neo-paganism as a solution to all modern ills. He was aware of the despair of many people's existence in an age when belief in anything transcendent – a Christian (or any other) God, or the Marxist concept of History progressing towards a distant utopia – had vanished. Central to his outlook is the concept of the Absurd.

'Everything that exalts life adds at the same time to its Absurdity,' he wrote in *The Myth of Sisyphus*, his philosophical essay published in 1943. Camus accepted that life has no absolute, eternally-grounded meaning to give our lives and actions significance. He calmly envisioned a future hundreds of thousands of years hence when humanity will have vanished from the face of the earth: Shakespeare, Michelangelo, the Pyramids and the Taj Mahal will all be erased or forgotten. This did not worry him for posthumous fame struck him as bogus. Faced with the revelation of humanity's cosmic insignificance, everyday actions or scenes, indeed all human efforts, suddenly appear absurd, totally devoid of meaning. Camus heroically rejected the easy option of nihilism – or suicide – accepting the absurdity of life in a world without a given meaning. Little wonder that he has been called (if half-ironically) a 'saint without a God'.

Was Camus an existentialist?

Camus hated being called an existentialist. In an interview in *Les Nouvelles Littéraires*, (1945) he said: 'No, I am not an existentialist. Sartre and I are always surprised to see our names linked… Sartre and I published our books before we had ever met. When we did get to know each other, we realized how much we differed.' But writers are not always the most objective or perceptive judges of their own work and there were personal reasons for such a disavowal, shared by other existentialist thinkers. Even in 1945 Camus was a rival, albeit a friendly one, with Sartre, a man who seldom inspired wide affection. After meeting Sartre in 1945, Heidegger denied he himself was an existentialist. Marcel, to distance himself from Sartre's thinking, also came to reject the term. Camus has at times been called an 'Absurdist', but there has never been such a philosophical school. (Kierkegaard is seen as the forerunner of both existentialism and the Absurd. Abraham's sacrifice of Isaac might be an 'absurd' act.). Iris Murdoch thought Rieux, the altruistic narrator of *The Plague*, 'the perfect instance of the existentialist hero.' Despite his rejection of the label, Camus was finally an existentialist, the most poetic of them all.

THE OUTSIDER

Camus' first successful novel *The Outsider* was written in 1940 while he was living unhappily in Paris, longing to return to the sun of his native Algeria. (Algeria was then regarded as an integral part of France, not a colony). Its hero Meursault is a young man working as a clerk. Tough and street-wise, much like Camus himself, Meursault is mainly notable for his failure to show any emotion. Seeing the body of his mother who has just died, he exhibits no grief but merely asks for a coffee and smokes a cigarette.

The next day, unperturbed, he goes swimming as usual before seducing a girl he knows at the office, Marie. When she suggests marriage, he agrees indifferently. Amused indifference is his normal reaction to life. Later, on the beach again with his friend Raymond and their respective girlfriends, he calmly watches Raymond beat up his own girlfriend before the two get involved in a fight with some Arabs. Soon after, Meursault again comes across one of the Arabs, who draws a knife on him. Stunned by the sun and heat, he shoots the Arab once, and then again four times, and is arrested by the police for murder.

Meursault is put on trial but, in a society as racist as French Algeria, a white man would not have been found guilty of murdering an Arab threatening him with a knife if he had expressed the smallest remorse. However, he tells the police that he feels only 'a certain vexation' about the murder. In court the prosecutor picks on his 'callousness' at his mother's funeral to show that he was 'already a criminal at heart', even 'morally guilty of his mother's death'. Not helped by a useless lawyer, Meursault is found guilty and condemned to death.

Meursault's crime is an *acte gratuit*, a gratuitous act, in the purest sense, but one for which he comes to takes responsibility. Sloughing off his earlier indifference, he accepts his destiny while continuing to live in an eternal present. Waiting in his cell he marks 'the summer evening coming on by a soft golden glow spreading across the sky'. At just that sublime moment the prison chaplain enters to offer his own banal brand of salvation and is angrily attacked by the condemned man for such impertinence.

Insight

In his preface to the 1955 edition, Camus wrote: 'The hero of my book is condemned because he does not play the game... He refuses to lie... so you would not be far mistaken in reading *The Outsider* as the story of a man who, without any heroics, agrees to die for the truth. I also happened to say, again paradoxically, that I had tried to draw in my character the only Christ we deserve.' Meursault's living and dying for the truth makes *The Outsider* a central work of existentialism.

Camus never intended Meursault to be taken as a role model for he is an incomplete man. If Meursault discovers his own integrity, it is as a figure from myth or legend. Sartre saw it as a 'novel about the absurd and against the absurd.' Iris Murdoch called *The Outsider* 'a compact, crystalline, self-contained myth about the human condition, as economical, as resonant as ... any piece of imaginative writing.' *The Outsider's* limpid style owes much to the classical prose of André Gide, an older novelist also interested in North Africa, while its vivacity and seeming simplicity reveal Camus' current interest in American authors such as Ernest Hemingway.

Camus and the Arabs

Camus has been criticized for ignoring the Arabs, who made up the large majority of Algeria's population, in *The Outsider* (and in *The Plague*). None of the Arabs involved is named and the effect the murder must have had on the victim's family is overlooked. Meursault has even been accused of voicing the racist attitudes of *pied noirs*, 'poor white trash'. But Camus' real views were far more nuanced than this. He was very aware of the sufferings of non-French Algerians as his journalism of the time reveals – for example, in his reports of a terrible famine among the Kabylian Berbers. The novel, however, does not include politics in its narrow if illuminating beam.

Camus wrote most of *The Plague* (*La Peste*) in 1941–2 while he was living in Algeria. He was actually teaching in Oran, the city in which the novel is set. However, the novel has no relevance to any recent epidemic in that port. What it reflects, if obliquely, is Camus' experience of the German occupation of metropolitan France and the resistance to it. He later returned to France to join the Resistance, editing *Combat*, the chief underground magazine. The book won the Prix des Critiques on its publication in 1947 and became a bestseller. It is considered Camus' finest novel, among the greatest written during the Second World War, its understated tone far removed from the defiant hymn to solitude of *The Outsider*.

The central character of *The Plague*, who turns out finally to be the narrator, is Dr Drieux, but it is a complex novel, using both direct and indirect speech. It starts on an April morning in Oran – 'a city without suspicions, a modern town' – when Dr Drieux sees a dead rat. That day he says goodbye to his wife as she goes off to a mountain clinic to be treated for tuberculosis. (The disease afflicted Camus also.) Soon hordes of rats emerge to die. 'From dark corners, from basements, from cellars, from sewers, they came up in long staggering lines to turn round and die near men... You might have thought that the very earth was purging itself, allowing boils and pus to come to the surface.'

When the rats stop dying, they leave plague as their legacy. People begin falling ill and dying in growing numbers, although the authorities are slow to react. Rieux befriends Rambert, a visiting journalist, Tarrou, a humanist and opponent of the death penalty, and Grand, a clerk who has spent years attempting to write a book but suffers from terminal writer's block. They form the core of a group of volunteers to combat the plague, soon joined by Father Paneloux, a learned and courageous Jesuit. Each of the characters reveals some virtue Camus respects. In their solidarity, no matter how unavailing, against the plague, Camus finds 'more to admire in men than to despise.'

As the death toll mounts, the town is sealed off, becoming an unreal city. (There are echoes in its nightmarish claustrophobia of Kafka's *The Trial* and *The Castle*, which Camus had recently read.) Soon the hospitals are overflowing but little can be done for almost all the victims, who die horribly. When anti-plague serum finally arrives, it proves mostly ineffective. In the cathedral Father Paneloux preaches powerful sermons on the plague as God's punishment for the city's sins, but falls silent at witnessing the death of a child. Then he himself dies, clutching a crucifix.

Rieux tries to maintain a professional detachment from the suffering he encounters, but on leaving the hospital once attacks Paneloux. 'Until my dying day I shall refuse to love a scheme of things in which children are tortured,' he cries. The novel is, among other things, an indictment of Christianity.

Insight

Tarrou, talking to Rieux, says that all that interests him is 'learning how to become a saint... But can you be a saint without God?' Rieux says that, 'What interests me is being a man.' To which Tarrou replies: 'We are both after the same thing but I am less ambitious.' In Camus' eyes, becoming fully human is a greater achievement than becoming a saint.

The death toll levels off in the autumn and finally begins to fall. Tarrou is one of the last victims, dying in Rieux's own house. Finally the city is declared clear and reopened to the world. Rieux, who learns that day that his wife has died, hears the rejoicing and 'remembered that such joy is always imperilled. He knew what those jubilant crowds did not know but could have learned from books: that the plague bacillus never disappears for good; that it can lie dormant for years and years in furniture... and that one day perhaps for the misfortune and instruction of humanity the plague would re-awake its rats and send them off to die in a happy city.' On such a sombre note the book ends.

The Plague is usually seen as a parable of France's occupation by the Germans, with Rieux and his co-fighters representing the

Resistance, the plague Nazism. Conor Cruise O'Brien called it 'a great allegorical sermon'. Some critics object that the reality of Nazism is ignored, the battle against an inhuman plague oversimplifying the problem of political commitment. However, *The Plague* is not a realistic but a symbolic tale. It makes no attempt to describe actual totalitarianism. While Communists had played a central role in the Resistance, none of the characters in the book is a Communist. All, like Rieux and Camus himself, are liberal humanists except Father Paneloux.

Arguably, there are only three fully realized characters in the novel: Rieux, the city and the plague itself, other human beings appearing two-dimensional by comparison. The plague deserves a star role, for it has long been seen as a symbol of evil beyond race, creed, sex or nationality. As Camus later commented, '*The Plague* can apply to any resistance to tyranny.' In his essays *Neither Victims nor Executioners* (*Ni victimes, ni bourreaux*, 1946) he stressed the sanctity of human life – he always opposed capital punishment – criticizing Stalinism as much as Nazism. 'There can be no objection to totalitarianism other than a religious or moral objection,' he said. More honest and courageous than Sartre in his gradual slide towards Marxism, Camus spoke from the heart of existentialism at its best.

Existentialism and the Theatre of the Absurd

Camus was not the first to write about the Absurd. The idea had been anticipated by Alfred Jarry (1873–1907), the eccentric playwright, poet, cyclist, alcoholic and artist who shocked fin-de-siècle Paris with his play *Ubu Roi* (King Ubu). Jarry launched on an unsuspecting world Pa Ubu, the gross, cowardly, murderous, foul-mouthed tyrant of Poland. In creating this repulsive yet perversely fascinating figure, Jarry was perhaps appealing to something excremental in the human psyche (the Id, in Freud-speak). *Ubu* marked the advent of the Absurd in theatre but it was not appreciated at the time. Its premiere in December 1896 provoked a riot – the opening word is *merdre*, very like the French swear word – and there was only one further performance. But the impact of Jarry's play – the first 'absurd' play, deliberately shocking an audience that had come for entertainment – echoed down the twentieth century. Cyril Connolly, the first English writer to translate the play, dubbed Jarry the 'Santa Claus of the Atomic Age'. That was in 1945, the year the atomic bombs fell on Hiroshima and Nagasaki.

Amid the mass slaughter of the First World War, the Absurd was reborn in late 1915 at the Cabaret Voltaire in Zurich. Tristan Tzara (1896–1963), a Romanian poet, helped found Dada, the most violent art movement yet seen. (The name, 'hobby horse' in French, was reputedly chosen by sticking a knife at random into a dictionary.) Dadaists attacked the war by attacking every aspect of a European culture that they felt had produced war. Blowing whistles, beating drums, dancing around in sacks wearing top hats, they created bedlam and exulted in absurdity. 'Everything is incoherent!' Tzara cried. 'There is no logic... Everything happens idiotically... Like everything in life, Dada is useless!' Dada spread to other centres – Cologne, Berlin, New York – before mutating into surrealism.

A proto-existentialist vision of the Absurd emerged in the tragicomedies of the Italian Luigi Pirandello (1867–1936). In *Six Characters in Search of an Author* (*Sei personaggi in cerca d'autore*), premiered in Rome in 1921, six characters from another play invade the stage during a rehearsal to become arbiters of their own fates. In Pirandello's masterpiece, *Henry IV* (*Enrico IV*, 1922), an actor playing the role of the medieval emperor Henry IV falls off his horse. When he recovers, he *seems* to think he really is the emperor and for 20 years is treated as such by those around him. Pirandello believed that it was impossible to establish an integrated, objective personality in a fragmented age. Pirandello's plays were among the first to question the author's traditional omnipotence.

Ionesco's play *The Bald Primadonna* (*La Cantatrice chauve*, 1950) heralded the true advent of the Theatre of the Absurd. Jettisoning conventional narrative, it stressed the impotence of language to deal with incidents so grotesque that absurd is the only term for them. In *Waiting for Godot* (*En attendant Godot*), premiered in Paris in January 1953, Samuel Beckett (1905–89) abandoned all plot, structure and dialogue to create a universe where humanity is utterly displaced. Two tramps (or clowns) Vladimir and Estragon, waiting for Godot who never comes, while away the time with meaningless yet brilliantly comic dialogue – anything to keep at bay the 'terrible silence'. (The critic Vivian Mercier praised Beckett for 'achieving a theoretical impossibility – a play in which nothing happens that yet keeps audiences glued to their seats.' [*Irish Times*, 18 February 1956]). Beckett's later plays grew ever more laconic, dialogue becoming so minimal that total silence looms.

Silence often dominates the plays of Harold Pinter (1930–2008), the British master of theatrical minimalism and the Absurd. Perhaps even more existentialist is the play that made Tom Stoppard (1937–) famous: *Rosencrantz and Guildenstern are Dead*, premiered in 1966. In it the two eponymous characters (very minor figures in Shakespeare's original *Hamlet*) wander on and off stage, lost in a void where they become so confused they cannot remember their own names and come to doubt their own existence. With Stoppard's works, the Theatre of the Absurd enters the twenty-first century.

10 THINGS TO REMEMBER

1 *For Sartre and Camus, fiction offered a valid way to explore existentialism.*

2 *In* Nausea *Roquentin realizes the final futility of most human actions.*

3 *In 'The Wall' the prison wall itself, against which the condemned will be shot, represents the fixed limit of human life.*

4 *Mathieu, in* Iron in the Soul, *finally achieves authenticity but only at the cost of his life.*

5 *Sartre's* The Flies *examines key themes of responsibility and freedom.*

6 *Meursault, hero of* The Outsider, *goes to his death happy despite everything.*

7 *In* The Plague *Camus thinks becoming human is harder than becoming a saint.*

8 *The idea of the Absurd was anticipated both by Jarry and the Dadaists.*

9 *Pirandello's absurdist plays undermine the author's traditional omnipotence.*

10 *In the plays of Beckett and Pinter, near-silence finally dominates the stage.*

Postscript: what happened to existentialism?

There are two approaches to this question. We could ask what fashions in philosophy replaced it, for indeed it had gone out of fashion by the 1960s. Or we could ask whether existentialist questions are still being asked, and answered, today. The first of these is the more straightforward.

The end of the existentialist party...

In January 2010 France celebrated the fiftieth anniversary of Camus' death with a heated debate as to whether his body should be exhumed and transferred to the Panthéon in Paris, the repository of the officially famous. The question has not arisen with any of the other philosophers linked with the movement, but Camus was always the glamorous existentialist. His death in a car crash in January 1960 was widely seen as marking the movement's end. Well before then, however, existentialism had been losing its appeal compared to structuralism. For 1960 was also the year that Merleau-Ponty published *Signs*, essays on linguistics, and Sartre produced *The Critique of Dialectical Reason*, which he called 'a structural, historical anthropology'.

In many ways, existentialism's decline was predictable. Unlike Platonism or Hegelianism, it had never proclaimed eternal truths. Its swift rise to fashion in the mid-1940s, when almost every artist or writer on the Left Bank (and many foreigners) claimed to be an existentialist, stemmed from the particular circumstances of the mid-twentieth century. In a desperate post-war age, the bracing appeal of a philosophy that challenged humans to be free appeared overwhelming. Existentialism's fall from favour during the 1950s was partly due to the vagaries of intellectual fashion and the rise of structuralism. But it also reflected a split among its leaders.

In 1951 Camus published a book that ruined his relations with Sartre and Merleau-Ponty, the existentialist giants: *The Rebel* (*L'Homme Revolté*). In it he attacked the idea of political revolution propounded by Marx and Lenin as the highest good, in which individuals become expendable items. Marxists' teleological approach – reinforced by a 'dark' version of modernism, whose origins Camus rather strangely traced to the Marquis de Sade, Baudelaire and Nietzsche – aimed at abolishing all inherited customs and values. This in turn removed all ethical limits on human actions, paving the way for dictatorships such as Hitler's and Stalin's.

Insight

In effect, Camus accused Marxism of allowing the ends to justify the means. This abolished any ethical restraints, denied the value of individuals, and licensed any cruelty in the name of an ideal future.

In place of such moral nihilism, the third section of *The Rebel* called for a reinstatement of ethical limits on action and reasserted the connection between personal rebellion – which Camus continued to exalt – and compassion for human suffering. Being ready to accept there are limits to action distinguishes personal rebellion from political revolution. Camus offered a positive response to the absurdity of human existence, based on an ideal humanism or 'Mediterranean thinking', while voicing revulsion at the mass murders many thought politically acceptable. (*L'Homme Revolté* also means disgusted or revolted man.)

Camus hoped that his book would ensure him a place among the ranks of great French thinkers. But he was savagely criticized by Francis Jeanson in *Les Temps Modernes,* edited by Sartre, for his superficial understanding of Hegel and Marx and abandoning the hope of revolution while offering no alternative. In response Camus attacked Sartre – who may have had no prior knowledge of

Jeanson's tone – and the magazine's editorial board as bourgeois intellectuals and Stalinists. Sartre replied in kind, accusing Camus of swapping his earlier belief in rebellion for fashionable anti-communism. The debate quickly polarized, becoming personal and embittered.

Sartre did not always give the Soviet Union unquestioning support – in 1947 *Les Temps Modernes* published an exposé of the Soviet gulag – and he never actually joined the Party. But as the Cold War worsened, with the Chinese Communist invasion of Korea marking the start of the Korean War, people were pushed into opposing roles. *The Rebel* won Camus fresh fame and new supporters, especially on the right. He did not relish the latter, for he remained a liberal socialist. Accusations that, while teetering on a perilous tightrope between Washington and Moscow, Camus always fell off on the American side, were unfounded. He attacked UNESCO for admitting Fascist Spain in 1952 as strongly as he did the Communists for suppressing the Berlin uprising the following year. But he was deeply ambivalent about the Algerian War of Independence, feeling sympathy both for the French settlers, among whom he had grown up, and for the Algerians themselves.

Meanwhile Sartre continued to 'privilege' the Soviet Union, meaning that he tried, against all evidence to the contrary, to see it as perpetuating the true revolutionary spirit of 1917–23. In 1951 he wrote *The Communists and Peace* justifying Stalinism and in 1952 took part in the Communist-sponsored Vienna Peace Conference. Even Merleau-Ponty attacked Sartre for 'ultra-bolshevism' in his essay *Adventures of the Dialectic* (1955).

With this preoccupation with Communism, and Sartre's attempt to give it a subsidiary place within a Marxist world-view, existentialism as a movement was already moribund by the late 1950s. For existentialists, the party was over.

In its place came thinkers who often disdained the title philosopher. Claude Lévi-Strauss (1908–2009) was in origin an anthropologist fascinated by the American Indians. Rejecting

the idea of the subjective Cartesian self, Lévi-Strauss proposed
a hugely ambitious theory of 'universal structures' based on
language and the structure of the human brain. He termed his
theory structuralism, under the influence of Ferdinand de Saussure
(1857–1913), the pioneer of linguistics. The publication in 1955 of
Tristes Tropiques (*Sad Tropics*, known in English as *A World on
the Wane*) made Lévi-Strauss famous. In *The Savage Mind* (1962)
he dismissed Sartre's humanism, writing: 'I believe the ultimate
goal of the human sciences is not to constitute but to dissolve
man.' Aiming to reveal the common structure beneath the myths of
peoples as diverse as the ancient Greeks and the Inuits, he rejected
the first-person framework and subject–object distinction basic to
Western thought.

Insight

Essentially, Lévi-Strauss saw human beings as almost
powerless products of their genetics, language and culture,
a view utterly opposed to existentialism's stress on personal
freedom.

Michel Foucault (1926–84) also spurned the name philosopher.
Rejecting structuralism, he at first called himself an 'archaeologist
of ideas'. He is seen as a founder of post-structuralism, one of
the first post-modernist schools. Obsessed with the exercise of
power, especially in a sexual context (he was a sadomasochistic
homosexual, a fact which increasingly coloured his work),
Foucault took Nietzsche's thought to alarming conclusions. His
first major book *Madness and Civilisation* (1961) challenged the
idea that the mad were 'ill' and needed medical treatment, claiming
that modern treatments were not 'scientifically' neutral but a
pretext for controlling threats to bourgeois morality, a charge he
followed up in *The Birth of the Clinic* (1963). Earlier, the insane
had been interned with the poor and sick, reflecting different
systems of power. In *Discipline and Punish* (1975) he examined
our 'gentler' modern ways of imprisoning rather than torturing
or killing criminals. Foucault argued that such reforms in reality
just permitted more effective control – 'to punish less perhaps,
but certainly to punish better'. *The History of Sexuality* was

planned as a huge work on ancient and modern sexuality, but Foucault only lived to complete the first volumes on the Greeks and Romans.

Insight

If Foucault embraced the existentialists' defiance of social convention, his concerns and methods were very different from theirs – exploring meaning in terms of historical context and development. Emphasis was now on social structures rather than the human individual.

Jacques Derrida (1930–2004) became a superstar of the intellect, a campus guru of undoubted charisma but hotly disputed authenticity. While influenced by Husserl, Nietzsche and Heidegger, he found the whole Western tradition bankrupt. This was not an original finding, but Derrida's reaction was. He claimed that Western tradition over-valued what he called 'phonocentrism', meaning emphasis on the spoken word, because speech is closer than writing to idealized thinking. (Such a claim might seem bizarre considering the huge amount of written material around in the modern world – more than in any previous culture.) One of Derrida's most quoted remarks, from *Of Grammatology* (1967), is: 'There is nothing outside the text.' The shock of his remark is qualified by his explanation that the 'text' includes the whole world. Like many of his statements, this is 'playful'. Derrida called his way of doing philosophy deconstructionist and he had a huge impact on the literature departments of many universities. Other philosophers were less impressed. John Searle, a noted American philosopher, voiced the thoughts of many when he criticized Derrida for 'deliberate obscurantism... wildly exaggerated claims... trying to give the appearance of profundity by making claims that seem paradoxical, but under analysis often turn out to be silly or trivial.'

Insight

Foucault and Derrida both attracted cult-like followings from the 1960s onwards, especially in the United States, making Sartre look distinctly old-fashioned.

If in the 'Modern' period artists, writers and philosophers explored the self-expression of the creative individual, Foucault, and post-modernism in general, wanted to get away from the human centre of creativity towards an appreciation of the role of the whole of society and culture – the networks and structures within which we operate.

Both structuralism and post-structuralism have endorsed the death of the subject – setting aside the very core of existentialism in favour of some sort of claimed objectivity. The consciousness and transcendence explored by existentialists was seen as a social product. Existentialism had been, in essence, a humanist philosophy for an age that faced unprecedented challenges to its humanity, as Sartre insisted in his 1945 lecture. There was a heroic seriousness to it lacking in the post-modernisms that succeeded it, where the dominant tones, especially in Derrida, are the sneer, the bawdy pun and the snigger.

Of all the areas where existentialism might be assumed to have a continued influence, the philosophy of religion is the most likely, for a religious view will need to embrace the key elements of freedom, responsibility and engaged living. During the 1960s and 70s there was a resurgence of interest in existential elements in the philosophy of religion and theology, moving it beyond the classic arguments for the existence of God and into a more open exploration of life and its meaning. Here the influence of Tillich and Bultmann moved beyond the world of academic theology and started to impact upon the lives and beliefs of ordinary Christians. This produced – albeit for a rather short time – a flourishing of new thinking and a radical re-examination of traditional beliefs, typified by the publication of the controversial book *Honest to God* by Bishop John Robinson.

Insight

Liberal theology of the 1960s and 70s was made possible by the work of the existentialists, for it not only used existentialist language (Being Itself, Ultimate Concern and so on) but also placed religious ideas and language squarely at the centre of man's existential quest for personal meaning and significance.

But that phase in religious debate did not outlive the 1970s, and today a textbook on modern religious thought may have no reference at all to existentialism. For students today, existentialism has been airbrushed out of a discussion to which it has a great deal to contribute.

Writing in 1970, Mary Warnock saw existentialism as having had its day, as finally collapsing into sociology and anthropology. More positively, John Macquarrie (translator of Heidegger and himself an important thinker in terms of the existential elements within theology), writing in the early 1970s, gave an overall assessment of existentialism. He concluded that it would continue to make an important contribution to philosophy, but acknowledged that it was difficult to say anything about existentialism as a movement, simply because existentialist thinkers were so varied. Any one comment could not apply to all and would probably be contradicted by some.

Perhaps that is why, as a name as well as an approach, existentialism has largely gone off the modern radar. But existentialism was never a single or coherent school of philosophy; its ending as a movement was as uncertain as its beginning, so even now an obituary may be premature.

Are existential questions still relevant?

Even if existentialism as a conscious movement in philosophy has largely vanished, existential questions and the issues concerning how to deal with them remain.

There is today a resurgence in interest in philosophy. Questions about the nature of the self – although couched in terms which existentialists would reject – are keenly debated. Ethical arguments continue to be of particular interest to students, because they relate directly to issues which concern everyone, whether or not they take a conscious interest in philosophy.

There are also two movements that seem to reflect the loss of overt existentialism within the philosophical world.

One is the prevalence of 'Mind, Body, Spirit' publications – most of which do not really count as philosophy, but all of which speak to a growing need for individuals to feel that they can give their lives some meaning, and work towards a positive future. Many bookshops now have more MBS titles than those on philosophy or religion. MBS may not give answers with which the existentialists (or any intellectual) may be satisfied, but it certainly addresses and shows the continuing vitality of existential *questions*.

The other is the rise of fundamentalist religion, where commitment is everything and logical analysis or textual study is irrelevant. There are two aspects to this. One follows from existentialism, in emphasizing personal commitment – a commitment that does not depend upon rational argument or intellectual analysis of beliefs. But there is another, more sinister problem. Religion, which the religious existentialists saw as a matter of personal engagement and the exploration of transcendence, has been made into a 'thing' – a factual set of propositions and texts to be taken literally. Thus religion is degraded into what Sartre would have called the 'in-itself.'

Fundamentalism is essentially a failure to understand the existential nature of religious ideas and texts. It takes them as literal propositions to be accepted without question. So debates between scientific fundamentalists and religious fundamentalists over what factual claims can be accepted totally miss the point about the human tendency towards self-transcendence and the need to find or give life meaning.

Insight

On the one hand we have an apparently insatiable appetite for books that promise to explore and expound the meaning of life. On the other, we have the avoidance of serious existential questions by retreating into the literal acceptance of religious dogma. The one shows the continuing need for serious discussion of existential issues, the other the danger of ignoring existential questions.

In the 1960s, the dominant tradition in university departments in the UK and USA was linguistic. Philosophers explored the meaning of terms and showed their relationship to one another. Ethics was not about discussing right or wrong, but merely considering how one might justify and explain the nature of moral discourse. It was assumed that philosophers would *not* engage with the issues that confronted most people most of the time. Existentialism was something 'continental' and therefore, for many, off the radar.

Yet, reading the classical texts of philosophy – from Plato through Hume to Mill and others – it is clear that in earlier times philosophers *did* engage with the issues of their day, challenging people's assumptions and beliefs. Language was their tool, not their content.

Insight

There were exceptions to this disengaged stance. Bertrand Russell, for example, campaigned for nuclear disarmament, and pictures of the near-revolution in Paris in 1968 showed Sartre and (rather belatedly) Foucault at the barricades.

Today the world of philosophy is very much broader. Philosophy, as an academic subject, maintains its intellectual rigour. But, to take Ethics as an example, the philosopher Peter Singer challenges moral assumptions about global issues and does not simply explore whether, and on what grounds, one might be able to make a moral statement. Outside the world of academe, philosophy has now returned partly to the streets, as it did with Sartre in 1945. There are philosophy cafés, where amateur philosophers meet to discuss topical issues, and popular magazines that may just as likely examine the philosophy of film or of science fiction, as feature articles on one of the great thinkers of the past.

And it is this engaged nature of recent philosophy that links it back to existentialism, since the most pressing issues today are existential. What should I do? What does it mean to be a human being? What values may I take as foundational? How do I affirm anything for myself in a relativist world?

In all this, there is a concern for personal meaning and significance – exactly what the existentialists were after in the heady years, when austerity was mixed with hope, after the Second World War. With hindsight, existentialism was a rebellion against a growing tendency to see science and overarching theoretical explanations as defining life. In their place, the existentialists wanted an awareness that was fully and practically embedded in life – a philosophy that would offer personal freedom.

At any time of change and threat, when people are confronted with the fact that life is limited and not always able to provide what they want – and particularly when simplistic global visions (the success of global capitalism, with increasing consumer choice for all; the dictatorship of the proletariat) do not seem to be viable or likely to generate personal satisfaction – people start to ask existential questions.

We have seen how Sartre, Camus and others expressed themselves as (or more!) eloquently through literature as through philosophy. The same may be true today. Indeed, if you want to see existentialism alive and well and vividly presented on the silver screen, just watch some vintage Woody Allen movies. All the dilemmas about what life is for, how to be authentic, how to relate to others in a transient world, are played out – generally by the character played by Woody Allen himself.

So perhaps, far from seeing existentialism as a feature of a particular historical period, when the world, reeling from the chaos caused by two world wars, tried to reaffirm the value and significance of the individual, we should see an existential approach as the *norm*. From that perspective, the discussion of factual evidence and the analysis of linguistic form become important tools used by philosophy, rather than ends in themselves. It is the existential questions – Who am I? What should I do? – that should remain central to the task of philosophy.

So existentialism is far from over. It is now a feature of our everyday thinking, not a theory within the confines of academic philosophy. Discussion of marriage and the reasons for marriage breakdown now focus on the nature of personal satisfaction, or what someone is looking for in marriage, or the dangers of one or other partner becoming fixed in an inauthentic role from which he or she eventually, in order to 'discover their real life', feels the need to break free.

This language, influenced by psychology as much as philosophy, is profoundly existential; it is all about the experience of being a human being and relating to others. Unlike the field of neuroscience, which attempts to give an analysis of the working of the brain in order to explain our behaviour, thoughts and wishes, most therapies investigate the engaged human being. They look at involvements, commitments, desires, plans for the future, at the setting into which the human being has been thrown by circumstances and what he or she makes of it.

All that, as we can now recognize, is profoundly existential in its presuppositions. For life is there to be grappled with and affirmed, there to be lived authentically, free from the constraints that society is all too ready to impose. And that freedom, of course, was the central appeal of existentialism.

Who's who

Beauvoir, Simone de 1908–86

Philosopher, novelist and feminist. Born in Paris, de Beauvoir was among the first women to study at the prestigious Ecole Normale. There she met Sartre in 1929, coming second only to him in the final graduation. She went on to be the first ever woman teacher at a boys' *lycée* (secondary school). De Beauvoir became Sartre's lifelong lover and companion, being influenced by him and influencing him. In 1946 she co-founded with Sartre and Merleau-Ponty the magazine *Les Temps Modernes* and from then on was active in left-wing politics, campaigning against the Algerian War in the 1950s and the Vietnam War in the 1960s. In *Pyrrhus et Cinéas* (1944) and *The Ethics of Ambiguity* (*Pour Une Morale de L'Ambiguïté*, 1947), the first existentialist ethical works, she propounded a less absolute form of personal freedom than Sartre's, accepting that individuals are also in part the products of their backgrounds and so not totally free to choose. Beauvoir was a fine novelist as well as philosopher, her novel *The Mandarins* (1954) winning the Prix Goncourt, France's top literary prize. Her most famous book is *The Second Sex* (*Le Deuxième Sexe* 1949), still seen as the first work of modern feminism. In it she claimed that men had forced women to assume the status of the Other (echoing Hegel), for the existentialist standard of humanity (the *pour soi,* for itself) is implicitly defined as male. She examined the ways in which women had consequently been forced into the subordinate categories of wife, mother, girlfriend, prostitute or lesbian.

Beckett, Samuel 1906–89

Playwright and novelist. Born in Ireland, Beckett moved permanently to Paris in 1937. There he befriended James Joyce, author of *Ulysses*, Sartre and Giacometti. He wrote most of the plays that made him famous in French. In 1946 *Les Temps Modernes,* the

magazine edited by Sartre, published his short story 'La fin'.
He achieved international success with *Waiting for Godot* (*En attendant Godot*) in 1953, a dramatic vision of the world in which mankind seems to have no place. A landmark of the Theatre of the Absurd and of existentialist drama, it abandoned traditional plot and characterization. Later plays became increasingly laconic and minimalist, often concerned with memory as in *Krapp's Last Tape* (1960), in which an old man listens to recordings he had made when younger. Beckett won the Nobel Prize in 1969.

Buber, Martin 1878–1965

Jewish intellectual and philosopher, contributing to philosophy, theology, biblical exegesis and fiction. He was particularly interested in religious mysticism and related this to the existential quest for personal meaning. His most famous book dealing with this is *Ich und Du* (*I and Thou*), written in 1922.

Bultmann, Rudolph 1884–1976

Protestant theologian and biblical scholar. He distinguished historical fact from the layers of religious interpretation and myth through which it appears in scripture. He applied Heidegger's philosophy to religious belief, emphasizing the significance of meaning and interpretation (rather than the acceptance of factual or historical evidence), and the need for a personal response to the biblical proclamation of salvation.

Camus, Albert 1913–60

Novelist and philosopher. Born to a working class family in what was then French Algeria and educated there, Camus' further studies were interrupted by tuberculosis, although he completed his dissertation on Plotinus and Augustine (both North Africans). Moving to Paris in 1937, he was active in the Resistance during the war, founding *Combat*, a flyer that became a daily paper. His first novel, *The Outsider* (*L'Etranger*, 1942) established him as a major existentialist writer. In it and later novels, *The Plague* (*La Peste*, 1947) and

The Fall (*La Chute*, 1956), and in philosophical essays *The Myth of Sisyphus* (1942) and *The Rebel* (*L'Homme Revolté*, 1951), he explored the concept of the Absurd, which was central to his thought. Camus defined this as the outcome of the gap between our innate demands for reason, purpose and justice in our lives, and the reality of human existence in a majestic but indifferent universe. From this clash arises a possibility of authentic, indeed heroic action. The 'hero' can be oddly detached, as in *The Outsider*, a self-sacrificing doctor as in *The Plague*, or a figure of seeming futility as in *The Myth of Sisyphus*. Sisyphus is doomed to roll a rock up a mountain each day only to see it roll back. Nonetheless he is happy and yet a rebel – the two attitudes common to all Camus' great characters. Camus was friendly with Sartre and de Beauvoir in the post-war years until *The Rebel*, which attacked totalitarianism of all kinds, was savaged in *Les Temps Modernes* by a protégé of Sartre. From then on the two men were enemies. Camus remained a liberal humanist – on the left in politics but a democrat – and his reputation in France faded during his last years. It remained high elsewhere, however, and he won the Nobel Prize in 1957. He died in a car crash in 1960.

Derrida, Jacques 1930–2004

Philosopher. Born in Algeria, he studied in Paris at the Ecole Normale where he met Foucault. Influenced by Nietzsche, Husserl, Freud and especially Heidegger, he published in the years 1967–72 three key works: *Speech and Phenomena*, *Of Grammatology* and *Writing and Difference*. They mark the birth of Deconstruction, a novel approach to textual analysis. This stresses the role of puns, metaphors and ambiguity, minimizes the role of the author and rejects existentialist concepts of human freedom. Derrida's good looks, unusual style of lecturing and vatic pronouncements made him hugely popular on US campuses. He was visiting professor at several US universities. Cambridge University's award of an honorary doctorate in 1992 caused an academic uproar, however. While some detect parallels between Derrida's word games and Wittgenstein's ideas on language, others see his work as essentially fraudulent. His greatest influence has proved to be on literary criticism.

Dostoyevsky, Fyodor 1821–81

Novelist. Revered as one of Russia's greatest writers, Dostoyevsky's exploration of the unrecognized motives hidden in the depths of the human soul make him a crucial existentialist precursor. Born in Moscow to an alcoholic doctor, he had early literary success but was implicated in a revolutionary plot in 1849. Arrested and sentenced to death, he was reprieved at the last minute and sent to a Siberian prison instead. The experience turned him from a fashionably pro-Western liberal into a far more original mixture of Slavophil, political reactionary, mystical Russian Orthodox (but not conventional Christian) and pioneering psychologist. His chief works – *Notes from Underground* (1864), *Crime and Punishment* (1865–6) and *The Brothers Karamazov* (1880) – went far beyond the nineteenth-century realist literary tradition. Nietzsche was among the first Western thinkers to recognize his unsettling genius.

Dubuffet, Jean 1901–85

Artist. Dubuffet had his first solo exhibition in 1945. His aggressive *art brut* (raw art) was even more radical than Picasso's in rejecting all inherited Western aesthetic values. He used materials such as sand and cement directly on the canvas to stress this ugliness. Such art struck many as supremely fitted to express the *angoisse* of 1945, the year of Hiroshima and the opening of the Nazi death camps.

Foucault, Michel 1926–84

Philosopher. After studying at the Ecole Normale Supérieure and the Sorbonne, where he heard Merleau-Ponty's lectures on the mind–body relationship, he taught in Sweden, Poland and Tunisia. Nietzsche and Heidegger were major influences on his thinking. Associated loosely with structuralism and post-structuralism, which displaced existentialism, he called early works such as *Madness and Civilisation* (1961) 'archaeologies', using used historical material to analyse the present. He helped organize the important Royaumont colloquium on Nietzsche in 1964 and held the chair in the History of the Systems of Thought at the Collège de France from 1970 until his death.

Politically active on the far left after 1968, he was also concerned with prison reform and attitudes to homosexuality. *Discipline and Punish* (1975) was a study of the birth of the nineteenth-century prison. Very popular in the USA, he lectured at Berkeley University and was writing a history of sexuality when he died of AIDS.

Genet, Jean 1910–86

Novelist and playwright. Abandoned by his parents and brought up in institutions, Genet became a criminal at the age of ten, and was frequently imprisoned. In 1949 he faced life imprisonment for repeated crimes until Sartre and other writers petitioned the French president for his pardon and Genet was released. By then he had written the novels *Querelle of Brest*, *The Thief's Journal* and *Our Lady of the Flowers*, all marked by remarkably beautiful prose and lack of conventional plot. As in his plays *The Balcony*, *The Blacks*, *The Maids* and *The Screens*, prostitutes, criminals and thuggish homosexuals are the chief characters, all depicted lyrically. In later life Genet supported many causes of the far left, including the Black Panthers in the USA. In *Saint Genet: Actor and Martyr* (1954) Sartre hailed Genet as a prototypical existentialist, who distinguished good and evil through his personal choices.

Giacometti, Alberto 1901–66

Artist. Swiss-born, Giacometti lived mostly in Paris. Influenced at first by the surrealists, his own unique style – isolated, stick-like figures emanating existentialist *angoisse* – emerged in the late 1930s. He became friendly with Sartre and sculpted several portraits of Simone de Beauvoir. Sartre's introduction to the catalogue of Giacometti's exhibition in New York in 1948 helped establish the artist's reputation worldwide.

Hegel, Georg Friedrich Wilhelm 1770–1831

Philosopher. Born in Stuttgart, and educated at Tübingen University, Hegel when young thrilled to 'the jubilation of the epoch', i.e. the French Revolution. He ended his life a bastion of the illiberal Prussian state. In between he had written some of the weightiest books in Western philosophy. Among his main works are *The Phenomenology of Mind* (1806), *The Science of Logic* (1812), *The Philosophy of History* (1818) and *The Philosophy of Right* (1821). Hegel was the first to grasp the historically conditioned nature of our thinking. 'Philosophy,' he wrote, 'is its own time raised to the level of thought.' He thought that history reveals a rational process of development which, if studied, allows us to understand our own nature and place in the universe. 'The history of the world is none other than the progressive consciousness of freedom,' he said. He predicted that freedom, once the privilege only of monarchs, would one day be universal among human beings through the ineluctable dialectic of the historical process. His thinking inspired Marx, Lenin, Kojève, Merleau-Ponty and Sartre, but revolted Kierkegaard, Nietzsche and Karl Popper. Popper famously saw Hegelianism as justifying totalitarianism.

Heidegger, Martin 1889–1976

Philosopher. Widely seen as a founder of existentialism despite rejecting the label, Heidegger is one of the most important but also most controversial twentieth-century philosophers. This is only partly due to his notorious links with Nazism. He influenced thinkers as diverse as Merleau-Ponty, Sartre, Foucault and Derrida but Anglophone philosophers can find his writings impenetrably obscure. Born in Messkirch, a small town in the Black Forest, he always remained attached to *völkisch* (ethnic nationalist) ideals of a rural Germany. After studying with Husserl, Heidegger had a brilliant academic career at Marburg and Freiburg universities. Among students overwhelmed by his personality and intellect was Hannah Arendt, who became his lover. In 1927, inspired especially by Kierkegaard, Nietzsche and the Presocratic Greeks, he published his masterpiece *Being and Time*. In it he applied the phenomenology learned from Husserl to ontology in an attempt to grasp the meaning of Being. He coined the term Dasein ('being there') to describe existence. His concept of Being as the main subject of ontological study led to a holism almost unique in Western thought, in stark contrast to the Cartesian split between mind and matter. Heidegger claimed that Western philosophy has, since Plato, forgotten what it means 'to be'. We are not separate from but embodied in this world, into which we are 'thrown' (*geworfen*) culturally, socially and physically at a particular time. Forgetfulness of Being is leading us to ecological as well as intellectual catastrophe in a universe without a god. A deep religious strain in Heidegger's thinking looked at one stage for a god in this world and in his inaugural address as Rector of Freiburg University in April 1933, he praised the new Nazi regime of Adolf Hitler. Heidegger resigned his post only a year later but long remained a Nazi party member, never really repenting his views. Banned from teaching in post-war Germany because of this, he found new followers among the French existentialists. The title of Sartre's *Being and Nothingness* is a tribute to *Being and Time*. But when Sartre visited Heidegger, neither was impressed by the other. In his later years Heidegger's thinking took a quasi-mystical turn, often seen as resembling Buddhism and Taoism.

Husserl, Edmund 1859–1938

Philosopher. Husserl was the founder of phenomenology, one of the twentieth century's most influential schools and the intellectual method chosen by Heidegger, Sartre and Merleau-Ponty to pursue very different goals. Born to a Jewish family in what is now the Czech Republic, Husserl was German by culture, studying in Leipzig, Vienna and Berlin before teaching at Göttingen and Freiburg universities. Attending Franz Brentano's lectures on psychology, he came to see science as complementing philosophy and did his PhD in maths. In 1900–1 he published *Logical Investigations* in which, following Descartes and Hume, he accepted that conscious awareness of objects is the one thing certain in life. He used the term *Lebenswelt* ('life's world') for the world we experience. For him phenomenology is an analysis of our subjective mental processes, which he called the 'intuitive study of essences' and summarized in *Ideas: General Introduction to Phenomenology* (1913). Husserl's star protégé was Heidegger, who dedicated the first edition of *Being and Time* (1927) to him, despite their by then major differences. With the coming of Nazism, Husserl was forced out of academic life and Heidegger disowned him.

Ionesco, Eugène 1909–94

Playwright. Romanian-born, Ionesco settled in Paris, writing in French. Founder of the Theatre of the Absurd, he won intellectual acclaim with *The Bald Primadonna* (1950) and similar plays such as *The Lesson* (1951) stressing the impotence of language to communicate except through often inadvertent absurdity. Made a member of the elite Académie Française in 1970, he won further awards, among them the Jerusalem Prize, in 1973, for his whole work. *Rhinoceros* (1959), the play which made him famous around the world, was praised as 'one of the great demonstrations against totalitarianism'. Its hero Bérenger has to make existentialist choices about freedom, authenticity and tyranny.

Jaspers, Karl 1883–1969

Philosopher. One of the founders of existentialism, Jaspers began his career as a psychiatrist, turning to philosophy after the traumas of the First World War. His great work was his three-volume *Philosophy* (1932) in which he explained his ideas of *Existenz* (he coined the term). Deeply influenced by Kierkegaard and Nietzsche, he posited three options open to modern humanity: to explore the world scientifically, which reveals, however, only relative, not absolute truths; to discover the self, whose *Existenz* is not fixed but is free to act unconditionally; and to approach the Transcendent, which takes the place of God in his philosophy. Jaspers was a friendly rival of Heidegger until the triumph of Nazism ended their friendship. (Jaspers had a Jewish wife and was barred from teaching by the Nazis). After 1945 Jaspers was an advisor to post-war Germany but he himself moved to Switzerland. He was first Hannah Arendt's tutor and later effectively her pupil.

Kierkegaard, Søren 1813–55

Philosopher, theologian, critic and psychologist. Born in Copenhagen, he was brought up by a gloomily religious father whose melancholy and guilt he inherited. His rejection both of

Hegel's philosophy, then intellectually dominant in northern Europe, and of the complacent Lutheranism current in Denmark led him to an intensely personal, ultra-protestant form of Christianity. He also hugely admired Socrates for fearlessly living and dying for his beliefs. He saw in the ancient Greek a role model for his own rejection of worldly success. In *Either/Or* and *Fear and Trembling* (both 1843), *The Concept of Anxiety* (1844), *Stages on Life's Way* (1845) and *Sickness Unto Death* (1849) he outlined his beliefs that every Christian must make existential choices that will lead to their eternal damnation or salvation. The supreme example of this comes in the Bible, when Abraham is prepared to sacrifice his only son Isaac in obedience to God's command, making the 'leap of faith' necessary to overcome the usual ethical objections. The phrase 'leap of faith' encapsulates Kierkegaard's belief that individuals must be seen as essentially moral beings constantly having to make personal choices. The tensions such compulsion generates can produce profound Angst, something from which he himself suffered. Kierkegaard is generally considered the first true existentialist and the greatest Christian existentialist.

Lévi-Strauss, Claude 1908–2009

Philosopher and anthropologist. A founder of structuralism, he started his career researching among the tribes of Brazil. Subsequent admiration for the indigenous peoples of the Americas led him to reject Western civilization's claims to uniqueness. Arguing that human social structures are much the same everywhere, *The Elementary Structures of Kinship* (1949) examined how peoples organized their families. *The Raw and the Cooked, From Honey to Ashes* and *The Naked Man* were among striking titles from his *Mythologies* (1969–81). In later years he accepted many honours from the civilization he deprecated, from a professorship at the Collège de France in 1959 to election to the Académie Française in 1973. Often cited by Foucault and Derrida, he clashed with Sartre over existentialist ideas of personal freedom but was praised by de Beauvoir for his radical interpretation of women's roles in human kinship.

Marcel, Gabriel (1889–1973)

Philosopher, playwright and critic. Although he disliked the label –
because he hated being classed alongside Sartre – Marcel is
considered the great twentieth-century Christian existentialist. He
provided Christian solutions to existentialist problems. Influenced
by Kierkegaard, whose work he introduced to French readers, he
preferred to call himself 'neo-Socratic', however. Born in Paris
to a Jewish mother and an atheist father, he worked for years
as a drama critic and wrote many plays himself. He converted
to Catholicism in 1929. In *Being and Having* he distinguished
between one's being and one's life: 'I am' is existentially prior
to 'I live'. His principal books include *Mystery of Being* (1951),
Existence and Freedom (1946) in which he challenged Sartre's
pessimism about the human condition, and *Man Against Mass
Society* (1955), attacking the dehumanizing effects of technology.
While Marcel's plays were not as popular as Camus' or Sartre's
fictional works, his philosophy, written in clear, non-technical
style, had great appeal to the laity.

Merleau-Ponty, Maurice 1907–61

Philosopher, co-founder of existentialism with Sartre and
'phenomenologist of the body'. He studied at the École Normale
Supérieure alongside Sartre and de Beauvoir, being much influenced
by Husserl and Heidegger. His book *Phenomenology of Perception*
(1945) both gained him his doctorate and launched his assault
on Cartesian subject–object dualism. He challenged Descartes'
famous dictum, 'I think therefore I am', declaring instead, 'I belong
to myself while belonging to the world.' Our body is neither a
subject nor an object. Our attempts to see the world as a detached
object must be mediated through the body, for 'the perceiving
mind is an incarnate mind.' In all his work he refuted the deeply
entrenched trends in Western philosophy towards either empiricism
or what he called intellectualism, more usually termed idealism.
He held the Chair of Philosophy at the Collège de France from
1952 (he was the youngest person ever elected to the post) until his
death. In his late essay *Eye and Mind* (1961) he used painting to

illustrate the body's relation to the world. A co-founder with Sartre and de Beauvoir of *Les Temps Modernes* in 1945, he edited the political section. He broadly supported the left, at one stage even trying to defend Stalinism. However, he later became critical of Communism and Sartre's drift towards Marxism and the two men quarrelled irreparably over politics. Their relationship had already become strained because of Merleau-Ponty's criticism of Sartre's metaphysical dualism and negative views on sexual relationships. Merleau-Ponty died suddenly of a stroke in 1961.

Murdoch, Iris 1919–99

Philosopher and novelist. Better known for her novels, she taught philosophy for 15 years at Oxford before becoming a full-time writer. Essentially a Platonist, she wrote widely and sympathetically on existentialism. Among her works were the first book in English on Sartre, *Sartre: Romantic Rationalist* (1953) and *Existentialists and Mystics* (1997). The characters in her novels often have to make existentialist choices.

Nietzsche, Friedrich 1844–1900

Philosopher, psychologist and poet. Born in Leizpig, son of a Lutheran pastor, Nietzsche was a precociously brilliant scholar, becoming Professor of Classical Philology at Basel University at the age of only 24. By then he had already discovered Schopenhauer's works, which had 'made him a philosopher'. Equally significant was his friendship with Richard Wagner, whose operas he hailed as recreating Greek drama in his first major work *The Birth of Tragedy* (1872). Forced by ill health to resign his chair in 1879, over the next decade he published a series of iconoclastic books: *Daybreak, The Joyful Science, Thus Spoke Zarathustra* and *Beyond Good and Evil*. In them he attacked almost all Western thinking since Plato and Christianity in its entirety. Nietzsche not only proclaimed the death of God and the advent of the Übermensch, in *The Genealogy of Morals* he exposed what he saw as the rancid foundations of Christian morality. As remarkable as his intellectual audacity was his psychological acuity, especially about women, but neither was recognized in his lifetime. After his death his unfinished writings were published in misleading form by his sister Elisabeth as *The Will to Power* (1900). He had a huge influence on Jaspers, Heidegger, Sartre, Camus and Foucault.

Ortega y Gassett, José 1883–1955

Philosopher. One of Spain's greatest modern philosophers, keenly aware of intellectual currents across Europe, he was an aristocratic liberal living through Spain's most turbulent years. Influenced by Nietzsche, in his major works *The Theme of Our Time* (1923) and *The Revolt of the Masses* (1932) he attacked Cartesian dualism. He declared instead, 'I am myself and my circumstances', meaning a thing is real only in so far is it is rooted in, and figures in, my life. The self is not separated from its surroundings. He had a significant influence on Heidegger and Merleau-Ponty.

Picasso, Pablo 1881–1973

Artist. Born in Malaga in southern Spain, Picasso came to Paris in 1900. One of the pioneers of cubism – *Les Demoiselles d'Avignon* (1907) heralded the movement's birth with its novel ugliness, brute power and abandonment of single unitary perspective – his art continued to evolve through the 1920s and 1930s. With *Guernica* (1937) he created the century's iconic painting, becoming a noted anti-Fascist. It also confirmed his status as artist of the century. A friend of Sartre and de Beauvoir during the war, Picasso joined the Communist Party in late 1944, an act that aroused debate about his authenticity and commitment. However, in 1945 he finally left Paris and its disputes for the south of France.

Pirandello, Luigi 1867–1936

Playwright and novelist. Born in Sicily, he became famous with *Six Characters in Search of an Author* (1921). In it actors from a different play invade the stage during a rehearsal to take control of their own fates after the author fails to complete their play – a novel concept of rebellion. In another tragicomedy *Henry IV* (1922), an actor grows convinced he really is the character he is playing. The play explores the impossibility of defining objective personalities for anyone, pointing towards the existentialist dilemma of authenticity. A supporter of Mussolini's Fascist regime, Pirandello won the Nobel Prize for literature in 1934.

Sartre, Jean-Paul 1905–80

Philosopher, novelist, playwright and critic. A giant of twentieth-century intellectual life, admired for his fiction, plays and philosophy, Sartre is one of the few modern philosophers to be widely known. After his father died early, Sartre grew up cosseted by his mother and other women. A bookish child with poor eyesight, he attended the elite Ecole Normale in Paris. There he met Simone de Beauvoir, who became his lover, muse and confidante. From 1933 to 1935 he studied in Germany, discovering the philosophy of Husserl and Heidegger, but he spent the next few years teaching in Le Havre, which he loathed. In 1938 his first great novel *Nausea* won acclaim but he was conscripted in 1939. Captured at France's defeat in 1940, he was a POW for a year, still studying Heidegger. Released in 1941, he returned to Paris and published his masterpiece *Being and Nothingness* (1943). In it he used phenomenology to express the core belief of existentialism: that in humanity, and in humanity alone, existence precedes essence. 'Thrown' into this world, human beings must accept personal responsibility for their actions without appealing to a god, party or church. In so doing, they create themselves. Sartre himself helped the Resistance by writing plays such as *The Flies* – set in ancient Greece partly to escape the censor – about individuals defying authority, both political and social. His play *No Exit* (*Huis Clos*) of 1948 coined the famous phrase: 'Hell is other people'. In 1945 his optimistic lecture 'Existentialism is a Humanism' (published as *Existentialism and Humanism*) inspired a generation and made existentialism the one fashionable philosophy. A co-founder of *Les Temps Modernes* with Merleau-Ponty and de Beauvoir, Sartre was always politically active on the left. This led to bitter disputes, famously with Camus in 1951, who disagreed with

Sartre's long if sometimes critical support of the Soviet Union. The two men, who had been friends, became bitter enemies. Sartre was also an original and perceptive literary critic, writing on Baudelaire, Jean Genet – whose freedom he had helped procure – and Flaubert. In 1964 he turned down the Nobel Prize for literature to preserve his moral independence but over the following years his support for ultra-revolutionary causes risked him seeming ridiculous. During the Paris riots in 1968, he supported the students openly. President de Gaulle declined to arrest him, saying: 'One does not arrest Voltaire!' In 1973 Sartre finally went blind – his health had always been poor, weakened by smoking, drinking and occasional drug abuse, such as his unhappy experiment with mescaline in 1935 – and he had to give up writing. At his death in 1980, 50,000 people lined the streets of Paris for his funeral.

Tillich, Paul Johannes 1886–1965

Theologian. Born in Germany, Tillich was among the twentieth century's most important theologians. Dismissed by the Nazis from his post at Frankfurt University in 1933, Tillich moved to the United States, ultimately becoming Professor of Divinity at Harvard. The existential themes in his theology are clearly seen in his most important work *Systematic Theology* (the first volume of which was published in 1951) and in *The Courage to Be* (1952).

Unamuno, Miguel de 1864–1936

Philosopher, novelist and poet. One of modern Spain's greatest intellectual figures, Unamuno came from the Basque city of Bilbao. He held the Chair of Philosophy at Salamanca (Spain's premier university) twice: in 1920–4, until he was exiled by the dictator Rivera, and again in 1931–6. The second period ended when he famously confronted Fascist soldiers in defence of intellectual liberty. Perennially concerned about the meaning of life, death and immortality, unsatisfied by scientific answers to such questions, in his best-known work *The Tragic Sense of Life* he called for an effectively existential attitude, for people to act as if human life indeed had a transcendent meaning.

Further Reading

In addition to the books by existentialist authors already mentioned in the text, the following is a personal selection that may be useful for those wanting to explore further:

Anderson, Thomas C., *Sartre's Two Ethics* (Open Court, 1993)

Barrett, W.C., *Irrational Man: A Study in Existential Philosophy* (Heinemann, 1961)

Bronner, Stephen Eric, *Camus: Portrait of a Moralist* (University of Minnesota Press, 1999)

Coward, David, *A History of French Literature from Chanson de Geste to Cinema* (Blackwell Publishing, 2002)

Cox, Gary, *Sartre and Fiction* (Continuum, 2009)

Flynn, Thomas R., *Existentialism: A Very Short Introduction* (Oxford University Press, 2006)

Goldthorpe, Rhiannon, *Sartre: Literature and Theory* (Cambridge University Press, 1988)

Gorner, Paul, *Heidegger's Being and Time: An Introduction* (Cambridge University Press, 2007)

Guignon, Charles, *The Cambridge Companion to Heidegger* (Cambridge University Press, 1993)

Inwood, Michael, *Heidegger: A Very Short Introduction* (Oxford University Press, 2000)

Kaufmann, Walter, *Existentialism from Dostoevsky to Sartre* (Meridian, 1975; rev ed, Penguin Books, 1988)

Kenny, Anthony, *Philosophy in the Modern World: A New History of Western Philosophy Vol 4* (Oxford University Press, 2007)

Levy, Neil, *Sartre* (Oneworld Publications, 2002)

Macquarrie, John, *Existentialism* (Hutchinson, 1972)

Murdoch, Iris, *Existentialists and Mystics: Writings on Philosophy and Literature* (Chatto and Windus, 1997)

Murdoch, Iris, *Sartre: Romantic Rationalist* (Vintage, 1999)

O'Brien, Conor Cruise, *Camus* (Fontana Modern Masters, 1970)

Reynolds, Jack, *Understanding Existentialism* (Acumen, 2006)

Rodgers, Nigel and Thompson, Mel, *Philosophers Behaving Badly* (Peter Owen, 2005)

Sartre, Jean-Paul *Existentialism and Humanism* (translated and introduced by Philip Mairet, Methuen, 1948)

Schrift, Alan D., *Twentieth-Century French Philosophy: Key Themes and Thinkers* (Blackwell Publishing, 2006)

Solomon, R.C., *Continental Philosophy since 1750* (Oxford University Press, 1988)

Warnock, Mary, *Existentialism* (Oxford University Press, 1970)

Wicks, Robert, *Modern French Philosophy From Existentialism to Post-Modernism* (Oneworld Publications. 2003)

For further information about books by the present authors, log on to:
www.nigelrodgers.co.uk
or
www.philosophyandethics.com
which has further information on books and websites for those interested in all aspects of Philosophy and Ethics.

Glossary

Absurd, the – a sense that the world is devoid of the purpose or meaning that human beings usually demand; also a key cultural aspect of existentialism in the Theatre of the Absurd.

Angst (*angoisse*) – a non-specific feeling of insecurity and anxiety brought about by the recognition of the fragility and temporary nature of human life.

Authenticity – the existentialist virtue of 'being oneself' and taking responsibility for one's actions, as opposed to adopting a social mask or blindly obeying social norms.

Bad faith (*mauvaise foie*) – used by Sartre to describe a situation or tactic in which one avoids personal authenticity and responsibility.

Being (*sein/être*) – the human experience of being in the world (as opposed to things, which merely 'exist').

Being there (Dasein) – used by Heidegger to describe a human being, engaged within (and therefore not separable from) his or her world.

Contingent – used of any being that has a finite life, dependent upon other things and therefore liable to cease to exist, contributing to making human life 'absurd'.

Dialectic – the process whereby a 'thesis' and its opposite 'antithesis' are resolved in a 'synthesis'; used particularly by Hegel to describe the process of change, and taken up, in materialist terms, by Marx (dialectical materialism).

Essence – in Aristotle's philosophy, an essence is what makes a thing what it is, implying that it has an established, fixed nature. Sartre rejects this, claiming that existence precedes essence.

Existence (*Existenz*) – used by existentialist thinkers to describe the engagement of a human being within the world, as opposed to the mere existence of inanimate objects. For existentialists, it is existence that makes us what we are, not some fixed essence.

Facticity – the given embodiment and circumstances that shape every human being's initial position in life.

Faith, *see* bad faith

For-itself (*pour soi*) – used by Sartre to describe a human life deliberately engaged with its environment, taking decisions and establishing norms.

Geist – used particularly by Hegel to describe the absolute 'spirit' of an age, embodied in the process of historical and social change.

Hermeneutics – the study of the way in which texts are interpreted.

In-itself (*en soi*) – used by Sartre to describe the life of inanimate objects, lacking personal engagement with their surroundings and having a known, fixed nature.

Leap of faith – used by Kierkegaard to describe the act of existential religious commitment, going beyond the security of knowledge.

Master/slave morality – used first by Nietzsche to describe two different sets of moral values, one (typified in democracy and Christianity) designed to protect the weak, the other vaunting the values of nobility and strength; also later used by Paris Hegelians such as Kojève.

Nihilism – the view that nothing has inherent value.

Nothingness (*le néant, das Nichts*) – for Pascal, simple non-existence; for Heidegger, the nothing which reveals itself in objectless Angst is central to our existence, which itself arises from the abyss of Nothing; for Sartre, that aspect of life that does not (or not yet) exist, seen in hopes and plans for the future. So for both Heidegger and Sartre humanity's radical freedom is rooted in nothingness.

Phenomenology – a philosophy, particularly associated with Husserl, which is based on a consideration of the phenomena of human experience.

Ready-to-hand – used by Heidegger to describe those objects in the world which are available to use as tools.

Responsibility – a key existentialist virtue, especially in terms of acknowledging one's own norms and decisions.

Ressentiment (resentment) – used by Nietzsche to describe the envy that motivates slave morality, opposing the noble values of his master morality.

Thrownness (*Entworfenheit*) – used by Heidegger to express the fact that we are born into a particular set of circumstances, not of our choosing.

Transcendence – the crucial ability to 'go beyond' oneself, used as a balance to human 'facticity'.

Übermensch – Nietzsche's view of the 'over-man' or superman; a higher form of humanity, seen as giving direction and meaning to human existence, an ideal to which to aspire.

Index